BIBLE PROPHECY HANDBOOK

ISBN 978-1-60260-874-0

Cover art (angel): Stefano Grassi; http://grassistefano.com; info@grassistefano.com

Published by Barbour Publishing, Inc., P.O. Box 719, Uhrichsville, Ohio 44683, www.barbourbooks.com

Our mission is to publish and distribute inspirational products offering exceptional value and biblical encouragemement to the masses.

Printed in the United States of America.

INTRODUCTION

Many people consider studying the end times a curious and eccentric pursuit. Perhaps they've been disillusioned by the precise predictions of "prophecy experts" and the constantly revised interpretations that fit every political crisis. But the fact is that we can't ignore what the Bible says about the end of the world. After all, our hope and vision for the future shape our actions.

In the absence of a specific timetable, how should we live in the face of Jesus Christ's imminent return? As you might expect, the Bible has plenty to say on the subject. And as you may expect, people have many different views on the subject. Through these ninety readings, you'll look at the end times through several different prisms, along with the scriptures used to support them.

Christians throughout history have generally approached the book of Revelation from four different viewpoints. Each view has its strengths. None has been able to argue the others out of existence. We must be careful, though. Each view can also be misused. We will never know the exact time or date of Jesus' return (Mark 13:32–33). But God does expect us to be ready for his return.

Look up and read the scripture passages presented. Consider the thoughts and arguments made on each passage. Ask yourself the questions. Then, determine how you can best live in light of eternity, accountable to God through his grace.

TABLE: TYPES OF END TIMES

VIEW	EXPLANATION
Futurist View (It's all in the future.)	Only the letters to the churches (Revelation 1–3) are directed to John's contemporaries. The rest of the book describes the end of history.
Historicist View (It happened in history.)	Revelation is a foretelling of all of history, from John's day until the end of time.
Preterist View (It happened in the first century.)	John was writing a highly figurative message of encouragement to fellow believers facing terrible persecution under the Roman Empire.
Symbolic View (It's all symbolic.)	John was writing a timeless figurative description of the ebb and flow of evil in the world.

Reasoning
Every generation can find reason to accept the possibility of Christ's imminent return, while resisting the temptation to set dates for it.
Every generation should note how Revelation accurately portrays the battle between good and evil throughout world history.
Readers throughout the centuries have gained comfort from evidence of God's power and judgment no matter what their situation. At the same time, we may conclude that John's writing, like other biblical prophecies, contains both immediate and long-term references.
Today's readers can learn lessons from the past, readying themselves for the future and focusing their attention on Jesus Christ today.

Day 1

THE BIG PICTURE

1 Corinthians 15:20–26, 28; Romans 8:33–34

While there is diversity among believers regarding the precise order of events in the end times, we all agree on the "big picture." Jesus changed the destiny of human history. Though his promised future reign is not yet fully here, his life, death, and resurrection are its guarantee. Jesus' resurrection promises his followers a future life (after death) where evil no longer exists (1 Corinthians 15:20–26).

After Jesus has defeated all of his enemies, he will return as the final Judge. He will hold all people accountable for their actions. On that day, Jesus will finally answer the cries for justice (Revelation 6:10). Believers know that when we appear before the final Judge, we won't have to rely on our own works. Our Lord and Savior will cover our sins and accept us (Romans 8:33–34). After establishing his kingdom, Christ will control everything forevermore (1 Corinthians 15:28).

Need to Know

- Jesus was called the firstfruits. The firstfruits were the firstborn of any family or herd, or the first parts of any crop. The firstfruits were seen as holy, belonging only to God. Jesus was the first of the resurrected souls.
- God claims us righteous through our faith in Christ. This is what is referred to as justification.

Think About It

- Do you fear God's judgment, or do you feel justified in his eyes because of his grace?
- When you think of being accountable to God, what would you most like to change about your life?

Day 2

LIVING NEAR THE END

Hebrews 11:13; 2 Peter 3:10–11; Matthew 28:19–20; 2 Corinthians 5:18–21

Believers should eagerly seek Christ's return, not the world's applause (Hebrews 11:13). Jesus outlined the signs of the last days precisely so that we will be watchful. Does your life exemplify Christ's love for the lost (2 Peter 3:10–11)? Are you spreading the Good News (Matthew 28:19–20)?

In this world we will continue to face struggles. Yet the fact that Christ has assured our future with him adds a unique dimension to the Christian life. Our future is already guaranteed—eternity with God. Because of that fact, we can reflect Jesus' self-sacrificial love without fear. We can spend our lives for Jesus' sake (2 Corinthians 5:18–21).

Christ is the basis for our hope in the future. As Christians, we eagerly look forward to Christ's future reign and seek to reflect his sacrificial love in our world today.

Need to Know

- Hebrews 11 is sometimes called the "Hall of Faith." People such as Abraham, Sarah, Moses, David, and Samuel all looked toward Christ's coming, even though it didn't happen in their lifetime.
- Reconciliation is actually an accounting term. It means to make both sides equal. When we take part in the ministry of reconciliation, we communicate God's grace to others who, like us, don't deserve it. Through that grace, God makes us righteous.

Think About It

- In what ways does your life reflect Christ?
- To whom around you would you like to spread the gospel of Jesus?

Day 3

SIGNS OF THE TIMES

Matthew 24:4–8, 29; Mark 13:7, 32, 23; Luke 21:25

False Christs, wars, and famines—these are the signs that characterize our fallen world (Matthew 24:4–8). We shouldn't assume the end of the world is near when false messiahs, wars, and famines appear. In fact, the end may still be far off (Mark 13:7). However, these terrifying events serve as reminders to us that we cannot save ourselves. Only Christ can defeat the evil that is rampant in this world.

God's coming judgment will also be preceded by falling stars, eclipses, earthquakes, and other catastrophes (Matthew 24:29; Luke 21:25). These natural catastrophes will constitute God's final call to repentance. National leaders will be confused. People will faint in horror.

Scripture doesn't give us these signs so we can calculate the year and date when the world will end. Jesus told his disciples no one knows the date or hour (Mark 13:32). Instead, he simply warned them, "Be on your guard!" (Mark 13:23 CEV).

Need to Know

- False Christs or antichrists have appeared since the first century. John mentioned in his letters that many antichrists had already appeared. These were people who denied that Jesus was the Son of God (1 John 2:18–22).
- Jesus gives two parables in Matthew 25 regarding the judgment of people's lives. One is based on the story of servants who have been left in charge of their master's money. The other is a story about sheep and goats. In both, people face a reckoning for the way they have "spent" their lives.

Think About It

- What are some "signs" that you see around you of the natural catastrophes described in today's scripture reading?
- What do you see as the benefits or distractions of trying to pin down the time of Christ's return?

SIGNS OF THE TIMES

SIGN
• People living as if God didn't exist
• Explosion of knowledge and freedom of travel
• Wars and rumors of wars
• Widespread acceptance of immoral behavior
• Vacuum in world leadership
• Increased demonic activity
• Widespread abandonment of the Christian faith
• Evidence of breakdown in families
• Spirit of selfishness and materialism
• General disrespect for others
• Human leader declares himself to be god
• People ridiculing God's Word
• Significant shifts in political power and influence

SIGNS OF THE TIMES

REFERENCE
Genesis 6:5; Luke 17:26–27
Daniel 12:4
Mark 13:7
Luke 17:26; 2 Peter 2:5–8
Psalm 2:1–3; Revelation 13:4–9
1 Timothy 4:1
1 Timothy 4:1–3; 2 Timothy 4:3–4
2 Timothy 3:1–3
2 Timothy 3:1–2
2 Timothy 3:2–4
2 Thessalonians 2:3–4
2 Peter 3:2–4; Jude 17–18
Revelation 13:3–7

Day 4

THE ANTICHRIST

Matthew 24:15–21, 30; 2 Thessalonians 2:3–8

Two decisive signs will indicate the end of the world is near. First, the antichrist will defile the temple ("the abomination of desolation"). After that, a period of wickedness and intense persecution of God's people—the Great Tribulation—will follow (see Matthew 24:15–18). Postmillennialists believe that Christ's prophecy of the defilement of the temple was already fulfilled when Jerusalem was destroyed by the Romans in AD 70 (Matthew 24:15). However, most Christians believe that this event merely foreshadowed the horrific events that will occur at the end times. In the last days the antichrist will desecrate the temple with a disgusting and blasphemous ritual and afterward lead a ferocious campaign against God's people. This time will be a period of great suffering (Matthew 24:19–21). His reign of terror will only be stopped by Christ, who will return in glory (Matthew 24:30). Paul also predicted that a "man of sin. . .the son of perdition" would appear right before Jesus' second coming (2 Thessalonians 2:3–8).

Need to Know

- From the earliest Old Testament history of the Jewish nation, God always required purity of worship from his people. This highlights the significance of the defilement of the temple, which is an act of abandoning the most sacred requirement—to worship God alone.

- The man of sin that Paul wrote about was also referred to as the "son of perdition" and the "man doomed to destruction." Paul noted that this person would eventually be overthrown by Jesus, but before that he would work against the cause of Christ.

Think About It

- What concerns you the most when you think about a world power—bent on working against the cause of Christ—rising in the end times?
- What efforts do you see in your world today that might represent the work of a kind of antichrist?

Day 5

RAMPANT EVIL

Matthew 24:9–13, 24, 37–39; 2 Thessalonians 2:9–12; 2 Timothy 3:1–5

Wickedness will become rampant in the last days (Matthew 24:37–39). Violence, hedonism, and arrogance will lead to a breakdown of the social order (2 Timothy 3:1–5). Jesus warned his followers that they will be hated by all nations and even betrayed by their families (Matthew 24:9–10).

In the last days, many who claim to be God's people will lose their faith (Matthew 24:11–12, 24).

Due to the increasing wickedness, "the love of many shall wax cold" (Matthew 24:12). Many will be deceived by false teachers who will lead them away from God (2 Thessalonians 2:9–12; 1 John 2:22; 4:2–3; 2 John 1:7). Jesus described all these signs to his disciples so that his true followers would remain faithful in spite of these troubles and catastrophes. Only the person "that shall endure unto the end. . .shall be saved" (Matthew 24:13).

Need to Know

- Jesus compared the last days to the days when Noah lived. In the book of Genesis we are told that Noah found grace in God's eyes. In terms of the rest of humanity, though, God was grieved, almost repentant of his creation (Genesis 6:6–7).
- These passages reveal the dark side of humanity that will be so evident as time grows short. As we endure these times, we should ask God to develop the fruits of the Holy Spirit in us: love, joy, peace, longsuffering, gentleness, goodness, faith, meekness, and temperance (Galatians 5:22–23).

Think About It

- How would you outline the false teachings you hear around you?
- How would you describe someone who has "lost his faith"?

Day 6

GOOD NEWS FOR ALL

Matthew 10:23; Matthew 24:14; Romans 11:1, 7–12

Not all the signs of the end times are terrifying and horrific. Jesus also told his disciples that the Good News of Christ would reach all nations before he returned (Matthew 24:14; Mark 13:10).

Jesus also predicted that the Good News will be preached to all Israel before he returns (Matthew 10:23). Jesus anticipated Israel's future conversion, thus fulfilling many Old Testament prophecies (for example, Ezekiel 36:22–32). Paul explained that God has allowed the non-Jews to come to Christ because of the Jews' rejection of him. Later, the Jews will also be saved (Romans 11:1, 11–12, 25–26). When Christ returns, Jew and Christian will finally be reconciled as part of the same olive tree (Romans 11:17–24). Many amillennialists reject this last sign. They see the church as fulfilling these promises, because they believe it is the true Israel.

Need to Know

- Christianity grew out of Judaism, which was both a faith and a lineage of people based on God's promise to Abraham to raise a nation from his descendants and to give them a land of their own (Genesis 17:5–8). Abraham's descendants, the Jews, have struggled throughout history to maintain their land and their very existence. As Christianity developed into a movement on its own, embracing all humanity, it could have seemed to the Jews that their distinction as God's people was being watered down.

Think About It

- Do you believe the gospel has been preached throughout the world?
- What do you see as your responsibility on a daily basis in spreading that gospel to all people?

Day 7

VARIOUS VIEWS ON HOW THE WORLD WILL END

Acts 1:11; Revelation 19:11–16

How will this world end? When will it happen? Will there be any warning signs when it's about to occur? These and many other questions have plagued diligent students of the book of Revelation. Revelation does give us some clues. It describes bloody wars, horrendous hailstorms, and ghastly plagues. In the middle of this chaos, Jesus, the King of kings, returns to the earth to save his people and pronounce judgment on his enemies (Revelation 16:17–21; 19:11–18). There's no question that Jesus will one day return to the earth (Acts 1:11). All Christians believe this. But exactly how Jesus will return and the order of events before his coming has been debated for centuries. There are four main views about how the world will end—dispensational premillennialism, historic premillennialism, postmillennialism, and amillennialism (see chart on following six pages). Each of these views differs in the order of events surrounding Christ's return and even the existence of events. Most differ in terms of when Christ will return in light of the thousand-year (millennial) reign, and whether that reign is a literal one.

Need to Know

- Revelation 20:1–6 is the primary text for the Millennium, the thousand-year reign of Christ. Some view this reign in a literal sense, one that will be experienced on earth. Others view it as a symbolic of Christ's eternal rule.
- While there are many different views on the end of the world, it will include both the gathering of believers and the reckoning of all people before God's judgment.

Think About It

- What are you most curious about in regards to the timing of the events surrounding Christ's return?
- How do you think Christians should function together in light of their many different understandings about the end of the world?

Event	Dispensational Premillennialism	Historic Premillennialism
Rapture	The church is raptured prior to the Tribulation and taken to heaven to be with Christ.	The Rapture is part of the Second Coming—when believers join Christ in the air to descend to earth with him.
Israel and the church	Israel and the church have entirely different destinies in the end times.	The church is the "spiritual Israel," fulfilling the Old Testament prophecies concerning Israel, though some are reserved for Israel itself.
Antichrist	The antichrist is a person who will appear during the end times to personify satanic power. He will make a treaty with Israel and then persecute that nation.	The antichrist is a person who will appear during the end times to personify satanic power.
Tribulation	The church is raptured to heaven before the Tribulation. Israel is converted through the Tribulation.	The church goes through the Tribulation.

Amillennialism	Postmillennialism
The Rapture is part of the Second Coming	Israel and the church have entirely different destinies in the end times.
The church is the "spiritual Israel," fulfilling the Old Testament prophecies regarding Israel.	The church is the "spiritual Israel," fulfilling the Old Testament prophecies concerning Israel.
The antichrist represents satanic power throughout this age. Perhaps a person, personifying satanic power at the end of our age, will appear.	The antichrist represents satanic power throughout the church age. Most biblical references to the antichrist have already been fulfilled.
The church goes through the Tribulation, which is a final outbreak of evil at the end of this age.	The Tribulation is this present age. Evil lessens towards the end of this age.

Event	Dispensational Premillennialism	Historic Premillennialism
Armageddon	Armageddon is the final rebellion against God before Christ establishes the Millennium. The church is absent during this period.	Armageddon is the final rebellion against God before Christ establishes the Millennium. The church is present during this period.
Second Coming	The Second Coming will occur in two phases. First, the church will be raptured. Seven years later, Christ will return to earth to establish the Millennium.	Jesus' Second Coming will establish the Millennium.
Resurrection	The resurrection will occur in three phases: (1) the resurrection of dead believers at the Rapture, (2) the resurrection of Old Testament saints and tribulation martyrs at Jesus' Second Coming, and (3) the resurrection of the remaining dead at the end of the Millennium.	The resurrection will occur in two phases: (1) the resurrection of all dead believers at Jesus' Second Coming, and (2) the resurrection of the remaining dead at the end of the Millennium.

Amillennialism	Postmillennialism
Armageddon is the final rebellion against God at the end of this age. The church is present during this period.	Armageddon is a picture of the heavenly Christ leading the church to victory over all its enemies through the power of the Good News.
Jesus' Second Coming will establish the new heaven and new earth.	Jesus' Second Coming after the Millennium will establish the new heaven and new earth.
One general resurrection of believing and unbelieving dead will occur at the Second Coming.	One general resurrection of believing and unbelieving dead will occur at the Second Coming.

Event	Dispensational Premillennialism	Historic Premillennialism
Judgment	Three-phase judgment: (1) At Rapture, believers' works judged. (2) At Second Coming, Gentiles and living Jews judged; only believers enter Millennium. Resurrected Old Testament saints and tribulation martyrs with positions in the Millennium will be judged. (3) At end of Millennium, unbelievers face white throne judgment.	Judgment will occur in two phases. (1) At the Second Coming, believers' works will be judged. (2) At the end of the Millennium, everyone will face the final judgment.
Millennium	A thousand-year period that fulfills Old Testament promises for Israel. Jesus reigns literally in Jerusalem. Curse is removed from earth. The church is in heaven.	Jesus reigns visibly on earth. The Millennium is for both Old Testament and New Testament believers. The curse is removed from the earth.
New Heaven and New Earth	New heaven and earth unite the two peoples of God—the Jews in earthly millennium and Christians in heavenly glory.	New heaven and earth introduce new cosmos without possibility of evil; God is intimately present with his people.

Amillennialism	Postmillennialism
At the Second Coming, all people will be judged.	At the Second Coming, occurring at the end of the Millennium, there will be one judgment of all people.
Jesus reigns now in the hearts of believers and through the church. There is no future literal Millennium on earth. This age ends with the Second Coming.	Jesus is leading the church in this present age to preach the Good News throughout the world. This preaching of the Good News will establish the Millennium on earth.
New heaven and earth introduce new cosmos without possibility of evil; God is intimately present with his people.	New heaven and earth introduce new cosmos without possibility of evil; God is intimately present with his people.

Day 8

DISPENSATIONAL PREMILLENNIAL VIEW

Zechariah 14:1–5; Revelation 11:7–8; Revelation 16:16

"And I heard the number of them which were sealed: and there were sealed an hundred and forty and four thousand of all the tribes of the children of Israel" (Revelation 7:4). The book of Revelation assigns the nation of Israel a central role in the events of the end times. In addition to describing the sealing of 144,000 Israelites, the Bible places several end-times events in the land of Israel: the two faithful witnesses will die in Jerusalem (Revelation 11:3–8), the armies of the world will gather near Israel in the last days (Zechariah 14:1–5; Revelation 16:16), and Jesus will return to the Mount of Olives (Zechariah 14:4).

Dispensational premillennialists take special note of Israel and its role in those final days. If Israelites are described as God's chosen people, why shouldn't the nation of Israel play a major role in end-times events? Dispensationalists believe the return of the Jews to Palestine, the reestablishment of the state of Israel in 1948, and its continuing prosperity in the face of ongoing persecution can only be explained as miraculous. They're signs that the end is near.

Need to Know

• A *dispensation* is a period of time. When we use

the word to describe a perspective on end times—dispensationalism—we are talking (at the most basic level) about an understanding of God dealing with man differently, progressively through different periods of time. An example would be the period of the Law of Moses, which was both affirmed and superceded by the grace that was revealed through Jesus Christ.

- A *premillennial* view is a belief that Christ will return to earth to gather believers *before* he reigns on the earth for one thousand years.

Think About It

- Do you see a distinct role between the nation of Israel and the church, or do you see Israel's role absorbed into the Christian church?
- What do you think the role of the church is in preparing for the end of the world as we know it?

Day 9

ISRAEL AND THE CHURCH

Daniel 9:24–27; Revelation 19:7–9

Dispensational premillennialists divide God's plan for humanity into several eras or "dispensations." God has separate plans for Israel and the church. Dispensationalists point to God's promises to Abraham, David, and others that Israel would be physically and spiritually restored in Canaan under the Messiah's rule. These promises to Israel must never be confused with God's promises to the church. In contrast to Israel's promised earthly future, the church anticipates a heavenly existence as Christ's bride (Revelation 19:7–9). Israel and the church will experience separate second comings, resurrections, judgments, and future blessings.

Dispensationalists believe that Daniel's vision in Daniel 7 describes a seven-year period of tribulation designed to bring the Jews back to God. In Daniel's vision, the antichrist first befriends the Jews. Then after what dispensationalists interpret as three and a half years (Daniel 7:25), the antichrist begins persecuting the Jews (Daniel 7:8, 20–27; 9:24–27; see Matthew 24:15–22). As a result of this persecution, Jews will begin to return to God.

Need to Know

- Throughout the New Testament God describes his people as both the *body of Christ* and the *bride of Christ*. The church is Christ's body in that the church is the physical representation of Christ in the world. The church is Christ's bride in that she will be joined with him in a great wedding feast in eternity.
- While we all understand the terms *trials* and *tribulations*, what we usually call the *Great Tribulation* is a period of trouble and persecution that will be a specific part of the end-times scenario.

Think About It

- How do you feel you are prepared for a time of tribulation and persecution for those of the Christian faith?

- How do you function as a part of the body of Christ?

Day 10

THE RAPTURE

1 Corinthians 3:11–15; Philippians 3:20–21; Revelation 19:5–9

Dispensationalists point out that scripture urges the church to watch only for Christ's return—not some other event, like the Tribulation (1 Corinthians 1:7; Philippians 3:20–21). As Paul writes, Christians await Jesus who "delivered us from the wrath to come" (1 Thessalonians 1:10; see also Revelation 6:16–17; 11:18). Simply put, dispensationalists believe that Jesus' return is imminent. He can come at anytime, and the church won't experience the Tribulation.

In the Rapture, all believers—both living and dead—will meet the Lord in midair and ascend to heaven. Transformed in their new bodies, believers will appear before the judgment seat of Christ for their rewards (1 Corinthians 3:11–15). Then the church as Christ's bride will enjoy the marriage supper of the Lamb (Revelation 19:5–9).

Need to Know

- The bride of Christ, the church, will be dressed in *white*. The Levites, worship leaders of the temple, also wore white linen. It was a symbol of holiness.

- The word *rapture* comes from a Greek word that means "to be caught up."

Think About It

- When you think of Christ's return, what are you most eager for or threatened by?
- When you think of appearing before the judgment seat of Christ, what thoughts come to mind?

Day 11

CHRIST'S SECOND COMING AND MILLENNIAL REIGN

Isaiah 2:4; Isaiah 9:6–7; Isaiah 11:6–9

At the end of the Tribulation, Jesus will return to defeat his enemies at Armageddon, bind Satan, and establish himself as king over Israel (Revelation 19:19–20:6). The Old Testament believers and the martyrs of the Tribulation will be brought back to life. Jews and non-Jews, both living and dead, will be judged to ensure that only believers enter the millennial kingdom (Ezekiel 20:34–38; Daniel 12:2–3; Matthew 25:31–46; Revelation 20:4–6).

During the thousand-year reign of Christ, the Old Testament promises for Israel will be fulfilled. Christ will reign from Jerusalem on David's throne, establishing justice and peace over all nations (Isaiah 2:4; 9:6–7;

42:1). No longer cursed, the world will be free from sickness and disease (Isaiah 35:5–6). Even the hostility among animals will cease (Isaiah 11:6–9).

Need to Know

- The Hebrew word *Armageddon* actually means "Mount Megiddo." Megiddo is a town in northern Palestine. Because of its location, it has been the scene of many historical battles.
- The kingdom of Christ—a literal, physical, military kingdom—is what the Jews have looked forward to since the days described in the Old Testament. It is the basis of their misunderstanding of Christ's mission, which was first to establish a heavenly kingdom based on his sacrifice.

Think About It

- What are any fears you have, or you think others might have, about the return of Christ?
- What is most inviting to you about the millennial reign of Christ as described above?

Day 12

THE NEW HEAVEN AND NEW EARTH

James 5:8–9; Revelation 20:10; Revelation 21:1–4

Dispensationalists believe the Millennium will end with Satan leading a brief rebellion against Christ. After he is defeated, Satan will be thrown into the lake of fire (Revelation 20:10). The remaining unsaved dead will be raised. Unlike believers, they will face judgment alone—without Christ. They will be judged solely on what they did while on earth.

God will then recreate the heavens and earth, eliminating any possibility of evil. Finally, he will bring together the believers in the heavenly church and the earthly Israel. The book of Revelation pictures the heavenly New Jerusalem descending to earth (Revelation 21:1–4). There, Jewish and non-Jewish believers will live with God.

Dispensational premillennialists repeatedly warn that Jesus could return at any moment. "The coming of the Lord draweth nigh. . .the judge standeth before the door" (James 5:8–9). Be ready for Jesus!

Need to Know

- The *lake of fire* is mentioned only in Revelation. It is the final resting place of Satan and those associated with him. It's probably the same place that Jesus referred to as Gehenna.
- *Gehenna* actually refers to a low valley bordering the

tribal territories of Benjamin and Judah in ancient Israel. Infant sacrifices were carried out there, so it was considered a place of great evil.

Think About It

- What does it mean to you to be ready for Jesus' coming?
- What specifically do you need to accomplish in order to be prepared for Christ's return?

Day 13

JESUS' SECOND COMING

John 17:15; Romans 8:17; 1 Thessalonians 1:10; James 5:7–8; Revelation 19:17–21

Jesus prophesied a future of persecution and catastrophe. This period of unprecedented evil will climax with the antichrist proclaiming himself to be deity, leading a worldwide rebellion against God, and ushering in a time of tremendous suffering and tribulation (Matthew 24:15–22; 2 Thessalonians 2:3–12). Historic premillennialists contend that scripture doesn't promise an escape from the Tribulation, but instead calls Christians to be watchful, guarding themselves against spiritual compromise (James 5:7–8). Although Christians will experience the same type of suffering Christ experienced, God promises to spare them from his wrath (John 15:18; 17:15; Romans 8:17; 1 Thessalonians 1:10).

For historic premillennialists, the Second Coming is a supernatural event that will occur only after the Tribulation. They see two purposes for Christ's return: He will come to rescue believers and usher them into his millennial kingdom, and he will come to judge his enemies. Christ will defeat the opposing forces at Armageddon, condemning the antichrist to the lake of fire (Revelation 19:11–21). This will complete the first stage in Christ's conquest of his enemies. Jesus also will raise dead and living believers. These believers will have new bodies and meet Christ in the air to accompany him as he establishes his millennial kingdom on earth.

Need to Know

- First century Christians thought it an honor to suffer as Christ had. Paul referred to the "fellowship of his sufferings" (Philippians 3:10).
- *Persecution* is suffering specifically imposed because of a person's faith. Persecution of the righteous can be found throughout the Bible.

Think About It

- What thoughts do you have about the fact that God does not promise an escape from suffering for those who follow him?
- When you think of being judged by God, what areas most concern you?

Day 14

JESUS' MILLENNIAL REIGN

Psalm 47:5–9; Revelation 20:1–3

Jesus will demonstrate his earthly rule by chaining Satan in the bottomless pit for a thousand years, preventing him from deceiving the nations anymore (Revelation 20:1–3). Premillennialists believe that the establishment of Christ's millennial reign on earth will spur the nation of Israel to turn to Jesus. Moreover, this millennial period will fulfill Old Testament prophecies of peace, righteousness, and extraordinary harmony between both people and nature—"The wolf also shall dwell with the lamb, and the leopard shall lie down with the kid; . . .and a little child shall lead them" (Isaiah 11:6–8; 35:1–10; see also Psalms 47 and 72).

Historic premillennialists assert that only believers will be raised from the dead to reign with Christ in the Millennium—the thousand years of peace and harmony. The remaining unbelieving dead will be raised to life when the Millennium ends (Revelation 20:4–5). At that time, Christ will sit on his great white throne to judge these unbelievers.

The Millennium will end with a daring rebellion against God himself. Satan will be released from the bottomless pit for a short time. He will deceive people and gather them from the ends of the world to fight against God (Revelation 20:8). But God will destroy these forces and condemn Satan to the lake of fire for all eternity.

Need to Know

- The Hebrew word translated as *bottomless pit* actually means "the deep." Some translations use "the abyss."
- The book of Job gives insight into God's dealings with Satan. It portrays almost a courtroom-like setting in which Satan contests God and his followers (Job 1:6–12).

Think About It

- What works of Satan have you witnessed?
- What fears do you have regarding wickedness in this world? What comfort do you find in God?

Day 15

JESUS' SPIRITUAL REIGN

1 Corinthians 15:24–26; Philippians 2:10–11

Historic premillennialists believe that Jesus currently rules as Lord in a spiritual way in the lives of believers and in the church. But Jesus' goal is to destroy "all rule and all authority and power" so that everything is under his control (1 Corinthians 15:24–25). Christ will conquer the antichrist, Satan, and then death itself. All creation will eventually acknowledge Jesus as Lord (Philippians 2:10–11).

Historic premillennialists believe that when the Millennium ends, the dead will be raised and every person will stand before the large, white throne of the Lord. This final judgment will determine everyone's eternal destiny, whether it be everlasting life or condemnation. Finally, God condemns death itself to the lake of fire. Then Christ reigns over all his enemies. At that point, God will bring into existence the new heaven and new earth. Creation once again will become whole. Evil will never resurface again.

Need to Know

- The first Old Testament evidence of the resurrection of the dead was in the book of Daniel, one of the later books written. Before that, death was referred to merely as the end of life without much comment on what happened beyond.
- Christ's resurrection gave obvious power to the understanding that our souls are eternal and live on beyond our bodies. This legacy beyond this life, beyond Satan's power and beyond our control, is the legacy of Christ.

Think About It

- What methods of operation in the modern world do you most look forward to replacing with the reign of Christ?
- What will life be like when justice is complete and death is no more?

Day 16

POSTMILLENNIALISTS

Matthew 13:31–33; Matthew 28:18–20; Ephesians 1:20–22

Christians who ascribe to postmillennialism believe that Jesus will return to just such a world—one that has been "Christianized," thoroughly changed by the work of the church. In summary, they believe the Millennium will be established by the efforts of Christians, and Christ will only return to the earth after the Millennium.

Postmillennialists believe that although Jesus is in heaven, he at the present time reigns as Lord over all creation (Acts 2:32–36; Ephesians 1:20–22). Since all power and authority has been given to Jesus, and since Jesus promised that he will be with his followers "unto the end of the world" (Matthew 28:18–20), postmillennialists contend that nothing can stop Christ's followers from carrying out their mission to evangelize the entire world.

The church is now gradually transforming society in the same way that yeast gradually permeates a loaf of bread (Matthew 13:33). Of course, the church's progress faces obstacles. Postmillennialists believe that John's vision of the Tribulation symbolizes the constant conflict between good and evil that has existed throughout history (Revelation 7:14; 13:1–18).

Need to Know

- The book of Acts is the story of the early church organizing itself to accomplish Jesus' commission to evangelize the world.
- The first-century Christians believed they were living in the end times just as many Christians do today. The fervency with which they worked is the same fervency with which modern Christians work, observing our culture and anticipating the redemption of the world.

Think About It

- How would you describe your hope that the modern church will "Christianize" the world?
- What do you feel is your call in the task of the church?

Day 17

THE POSTMILLENNIUM

Isaiah 2:4; Revelation 20:4–6

Postmillennialists believe that the Millennium will occur within human history. The psalmist's vision that one day all nations will sing God's praise, that righteousness will flourish, and that true justice will reign will be fulfilled in our present age (Psalm 47; 72). The Good News of Christ has the power not only to bring about personal change, but social and cultural transformation as well. Swords will be hammered into plowshares (Isaiah 2:4), the desert will spring to life (Isaiah 35:1, 7), and Satan will be bound (Revelation 20:1–3).

Postmillennialists believe that this golden age of righteousness and prosperity will result not from Christ's visible earthly reign but from his invisible spiritual reign from heaven through his word (Revelation 19:11–21; 20:4–6). The Millennium will result from historical forces that are present now—not from cataclysmic or miraculous events. Similarly, postmillennialists interpret the "first resurrection" not as a promise that martyrs will receive new bodies, but that their cause in spreading the Good News will triumph (Revelation 20:4–6). They insist that the thousand years in Revelation 20:2 are symbolic of a perfect time—one that may last more than a thousand years.

Need to Know

- Numbers are often used symbolically in scripture because that is how they were used in the ancient world. When Jesus told Peter to forgive someone seventy times seven times, he wasn't limiting forgiveness to 490 encounters. He was saying, "keep on forgiving indefinitely."
- In the late 1800s the Social Gospel movement combined social justice with the spread of the gospel. Current thinking often has us choose between the two rather than seeing Christ's holistic redemption.

Think About It

- How is your faith making the world around you a better place?
- What does it mean to you to see yourself as a part of God's redemptive work in the world?

Day 18

JESUS' SECOND COMING

Revelation 20:7–10; Revelation 21:1–4

Postmillennialists believe that the Millennium will end when Satan is released from the bottomless pit to launch a brief offensive (Revelation 20:7–10), then Christ will return to judge all people. Upon his return, the dead will be raised to face judgment (John 5:28–29). Christ will establish a new heaven and new earth, where evil will no longer exist (Revelation 21:1–22:5).

Postmillennialists are optimistic about the future of humanity only because Jesus Christ has changed the destiny of history. They believe the church bears the awesome responsibility of spreading the Good News to all the world. And it's the church's commitment to tell others about Jesus that will bring about that idyllic period of peace and prosperity—the Millennium.

Need to Know

- As early as the writings of the Old Testament prophet Isaiah, we can find the concept of the new heavens and new earth (Isaiah 65:17; 66:22). God promised redemption and restoration not just for his people, but for the world.
- In Jesus' closing remarks before his ascension, he gave the directive for his followers to spread the news of the gospel throughout the earth (Acts 1:8).

Think About It

- How does your optimism about the future of humanity compare to that of the postmillennialist?
- What problems, if any, do you have with this view of Christ's reign?

Day 19

AMILLENNIALISTS AND THE KINGDOM OF GOD

Luke 22:29; John 18:36; Acts 3:19–21; Galatians 1:4; Ephesians 1:20–23

Amillennialists see the Millennium as Christ's current reign over his church. They point out that the New Testament speaks of only two different ages—this present world and the world to come (Matthew 12:32; Mark 10:30; Luke 18:30; 20:34, John 16:11; Acts 3:19–21; 2 Corinthians 4:4; Hebrews 6:5). Because

Satan is the "prince of this world" (John 16:11), the people of this age follow their worldly desires (Ephesians 2:2). In the world to come sinners will be punished for their evil, and the righteous will live forever (Matthew 12:36; 25:31–46). The event that divides these two ages is Christ's second coming.

Amillennialists believe that Jesus' work on the cross two thousand years ago established the kingdom of God. As a result, this "present evil world" (Galatians 1:4) is now passing away (1 Corinthians 7:31). Jesus bound Satan (Matthew 12:29), curtailing his power (Luke 10:17–19). Therefore, the "prince of this world" cannot prevent the spread of the Good News of Christ (Matthew 16:18). Jesus is now Lord, reigning as king in the hearts of believers (Luke 22:29; John 18:36; Ephesians 1:20–23). That's how Christ rules today. His kingdom is spiritual; it is the church.

Need to Know

- Jesus compared the kingdom of God to many things such as leaven, a grain of mustard seed, a treasure, a net, a marriage, and maidens waiting for the bridegroom (Matthew 13; Luke 13).
- Jesus' work on the cross was the redemption of humanity. Through his death, he paid for sin in the lives of people and provided a connection between God and humanity.

Think About It

- How would you define the kingdom of God?
- Do you believe you are already in that kingdom, or that you are waiting to be a part of it in eternity?

Timeline for the

Jesus is now Lord

Jesus' Resurrection

Church Age

Church Age

- Jesus reigns in heaven, in the church, and in the hearts of believers.
- The millennium is now.
- Satan cannot stop the spread of the Good News.
- Hostility to Christians will gradually increase during the Church Age.

Amillennial View

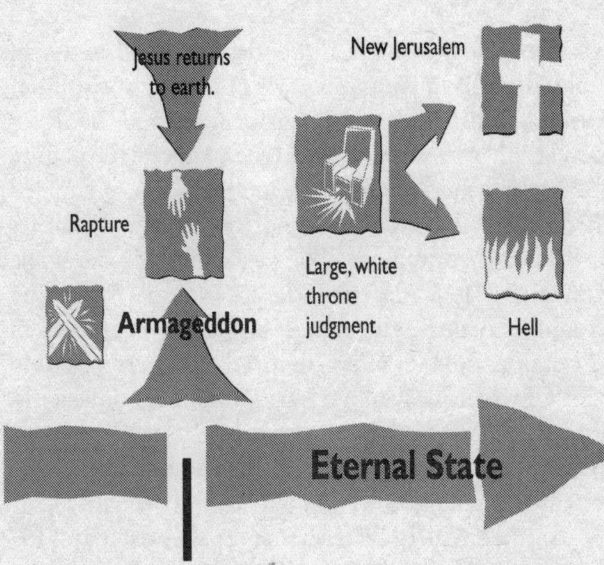

Christ's Second Coming

- Believers meet Jesus in midair.
- Believers descend with Christ to earth.
- Jesus defeats the antichrist at Armageddon.
- Jesus holds everyone accountable at the large, white throne judgment.

Eternity

- Believers go to the New Jerusalem.
- Unbelievers go to hell.

Day 20

A FUTURE MILLENNIUM AND THE END OF THIS AGE

John 5:28–29; 2 Thessalonians 2:1–3; Revelation 20:4–6

Amillennialists insist that the idea of a thousand-year "golden era" is incompatible with this evil world. They believe that the various visions in the book of Revelation run parallel with each other (Revelation 5–20). In other words, Revelation is not organized chronologically. Each vision portrays spiritual realities in the *entire* church age. The last section of the book, Revelation 21–22, describes the age to come. According to amillennialists, the first resurrection described in Revelation 20:4–6 refers to dead believers reigning with Christ in heaven. After all, John sees only souls, not resurrected bodies, in this text. So the events of the Millennium described in Revelation 20:1–6 are actually occurring now!

Amillennialists believe that as the last days approach, the forces of evil will climax with the antichrist and the tribulation he brings (2 Thessalonians 2:1–3). On the "day of the Lord," Christ will descend to earth, gather those who belong to him, and raise the dead. At this glorious return, everyone will appear before the judgment seat of Christ. The righteous will be raised to life, and the wicked to judgment (John 5:28–29). Those who belong to Christ will live with him in everlasting glory.

Need to Know

- The phrase the "day of the Lord" is used throughout scripture, as early as the eighth-century BC prophet, Amos. It points to *the* day, as well as any day, that the Lord intervenes in history. Most often that intervention has to do with judgment, an accounting.
- A judgment seat was literally the place where a judge sat. Pilate was sitting on his judgment seat when his wife warned him about Jesus (Matthew 27:19). The judgment seat of Christ represents not so much a place, as the absolute accountability that Christians will have before God.

Think About It

- What do you see as your role today in the kingdom of God?
- What does the hope of Christ's return offer to your life right now?

Day 21

WHAT ABOUT ISRAEL?

Acts 2:33–36; Romans 2:28–29; Galatians 3:29

What about God's covenant with Israel? Isn't God faithful to his promises to Israel—for instance, that David's throne would be established forever? Amillennialists believe that the church—the true Israel—will fulfill these promises. Paul and John state that believers in Christ are Abraham's seed—the true Jews—and therefore heirs of God's promises (Romans 2:28–29; Galatians 3:29; Revelation 2:9; 3:9). Peter claims that the resurrected and ascended Jesus is now enthroned, fulfilling God's promise to David (Acts 2:33–36).

Where is the church's promised Jerusalem? It is the New Jerusalem that descends from heaven in Revelation's grand vision of the new heaven and new earth (Revelation 21–22; see Galatians 4:25–26; Hebrews 12:22–23). Here evil can never exist. "Water of life" flows from the Lamb's throne, symbolizing God's intimate presence with his people. So amillennialists insist the church has displaced Israel.

Amillennialism presents the most straightforward view of the end times. On this earth, the wicked will continue to gather strength, persecuting believers more and more. Only when Christ returns will wickedness be stopped once and for all. After judging both the living and dead, Christ will establish his everlasting reign of peace.

Need to Know

- The Old Testament is the story of the nation of Israel. It is the backdrop of the New Testament in which Jesus' very existence was interpreted through God's promise to Israel of a Messiah.
- God made many promises about the restoration of Israel. That's why the fate of Israel matters in any view of the end times. How will God fulfill those promises that have been made since ancient history?

Think About It

- What is the task of the church today?
- What is the responsibility of the church, if any, toward the descendants of Abraham?

Day 22

DANIEL'S SEVENTY WEEKS

Daniel 9:24–27; Matthew 24:21–22

Jesus described to his disciples a period of terrible suffering that would precede his second coming (Matthew 24:21–22). The disciples knew about this period of intense suffering—the Tribulation. Although a host of experts have tried to map out what will occur in the Tribulation, we don't know much more about this time than Jesus' disciples did two thousand years ago. Each expert—whether dispensationalist, premillennialist, or amillennialist—has his or her own unique interpretation of the events.

A discussion of the Tribulation usually begins with Daniel's prophecies of the seventy time periods, or "seventy weeks" (Daniel 9:24–27). For dispensational premillennialists, the prophecy of the seventieth week sets the framework for the Tribulation. It's in that "week" that Daniel predicts the establishment of what one translation of the Bible calls the "disgusting things" and another calls the "abomination of desolation" (Daniel 9:27). Many dispensationalists believe the antichrist will set up disgusting sacrilegious things in the rebuilt temple in Jerusalem, and for this reason and others they understand Daniel's prophecy as predicting a seven-year period of tribulation.

Need to Know

- Most agree that the "abomination of desolation" will be an object set up for people to worship in place of God.
- While we think of a week as seven days, the "weeks" Daniel referred to could be years or sets of years.

Think About It

- How important does it seem to you to understand more about the possible anatomy of the Tribulation? Why?
- Why do you think, in God's scheme of things, the details can seem so unclear about all this?

Day 23

RAPTURE, JUDGMENTS, ARMAGEDDON

Revelation 9:20–21, Revelation 16:12–16

Depending on whether you are a pretribulationist, midtribulationist, or posttribulationist, the Rapture will occur either at the beginning, middle, or end of the Tribulation. It's within those seven awful years of tribulation that many dispensationalists place Revelation's seven seal, trumpet, and bowl judgments; everything from the sun turning dark to a plague of painful boils occurs during these dreadful seven years. But even though a third of the earth will be completely devastated in seven short years, people will still refuse to turn to God (Revelation 9:20–21). They will gather together at Armageddon to fight against the Almighty (Revelation 16:12–16). It's at that time that Christ will appear to defeat his enemies and to set the stage for his final judgment. The details of all these events—how they will be fulfilled and when—are still being debated. No one knows exactly what will happen. Scripture does make it clear that though we may experience troubles on this earth, Jesus will ultimately rescue his people from their persecutors (1 Thessalonians 1:10).

Need to Know

- The Tribulation is generally agreed to be seven years divided in half by significant events. The disagreement described above is at what point, in relation to the Tribulation, Jesus will "take up" the believers from the struggle.

- In John's vision judgments were poured out on the earth. First, seals were broken, some of which were followed by horses of symbolic colors. Other judgments were heralded by trumpets, then poured out from bowls or vials.

Think About It

- From what you've read and studied, are you a pre-, post-, or mid-tribulationist? Why?
- What have you faced or witnessed in your life that shows that people can experience events convincing them of God's presence, yet still turn against him?

Day 24

WHY WORRY ABOUT THE TRIBULATION?

Daniel 12:1; 2 Thessalonians 1:6–10; Revelation 3:10; Revelation 7:14

How would you like to live in a world plagued by catastrophes? A great earthquake? Meteorites falling to the earth? Fiery hail? And on top of that, all kinds of violence—skirmishes, battles, and wars?

The Bible speaks of just that type of terrible suffering—a period of evil unequaled in all of history

(Daniel 12:1; Matthew 24:16–22; 2 Thessalonians 2:3–12; Revelation 7:14). It's the time when God's wrath will be unleashed against his enemies (2 Thessalonians 1:6–10; Revelation 6:1–17). Revelation describes this period when God orders his bowls of wrath to be poured on the world as a time of testing (Revelation 3:10; 8:1–9:21; 16:1–21).

While most Christians acknowledge the reality of the Tribulation, there is still considerable debate concerning when it will occur and who will be affected by it.

Need to Know

- Throughout history, the Jews interpreted God's love for them, in part, by his vengeance on their enemies. John represents God as this kind of champion as well.
- Michael, an archangel that appeared to Daniel, is also mentioned in Jude 1:9 (as the archangel) and in Revelation 12:7 (as a warring angel).

Think About It

- How do you think your faith would hold up in a time of great testing?
- What kind of work does God do in your life when you face a horrible struggle?

Day 25

DISPENSATIONAL PREMILLENNIAL VIEW OF ISRAEL

Daniel 7:25–27, Matthew 24:29–31
1 Thessalonians 1:10

Dispensational premillennialists believe that Jesus' prophecy of a future tribulation will affect Israel, not the church. They point out that the antichrist is an integral part of Daniel's prophecy concerning the seventieth week, and according to dispensationalists, this prophecy only deals with God's plans for Israel (Daniel 9:27; Matthew 24:15–22). So according to the dispensational view, believers won't have to go through the Tribulation. Jesus will rescue them "from the wrath to come" (1 Thessalonians 1:10). Prior to the Tribulation, the church will be raptured out of the world when Christ suddenly descends from the clouds.

The rise of the antichrist begins a seven-year period of tribulation designed to bring Israel back to God. In Daniel's seventieth week, the antichrist first befriends Israel. Then after three and a half years, the antichrist blasphemes the all-powerful God by placing a sacrilegious thing in the temple. Afterward, he persecutes the Jews with vengeance (Daniel 7:8, 20–27; 9:24–27; Matthew 24:15–22). During this period of unspeakable suffering, many Jews recognize Christ as the Messiah and begin to turn back to God. After these seven years of horror, Christ returns to defeat his enemies at Armageddon and begin his thousand-year reign of peace (Matthew 24:29–31).

Need to Know

- The Jews of Jesus' day rejected him as Messiah for a variety of reasons, but perhaps most of all because he didn't bring the earthly kingdom they expected from the champion God had promised to send. Today, Jews who have come to believe in Jesus are often called *Messianic* Jews.
- After Pentecost, when Christianity was first growing as a movement, it was a Jewish movement. As the early leaders decided that a person didn't have to become a Jew to become a Christian, the two became more separate.

Think About It

- Do you believe that God still has a separate plan for the Jews (as presented in the Old Testament) or that the Christian church now represents "God's chosen people" the way the Jewish nation once did?
- What signs or events do you see around you now that could represent a coming period of tribulation or persecution?

Day 26

HISTORIC PREMILLENNIAL VIEW

2 Thessalonians 2:3–12

Historic premillennialists see the Tribulation as the climactic manifestation of evil at the end of history. During that time the antichrist will proclaim himself to be God and launch a worldwide campaign of persecution of Christians (Matthew 24:15–22; 2 Thessalonians 2:3–12). According to historic premillennialists, Christians will go through this tribulation and will suffer for the cause of Jesus, but Jesus will sustain his people and protect them from God's dreadful judgments on the antichrist and his followers. Then at the height of this period of persecution, Christ will return to defeat his enemies at Armageddon and establish his thousand-year reign.

Need to Know

- Persecution was a familiar concept to the early Christians. Jesus' followers had been persecuted from the beginning of the Christian movement. In fact, at times they were charged with and persecuted for atheism, because they failed to recognize *all* the gods of the day.

- Saul of Tarsus, who later became Paul the apostle, was one of the original first-century bounty hunters looking for and putting to death any rogue Christians out spreading the word. After his conversion, Paul became a martyr for the faith he once tried to obliterate.

Think About It

- What persecution have you experienced or witnessed?
- What type of persecution do you fear the most?

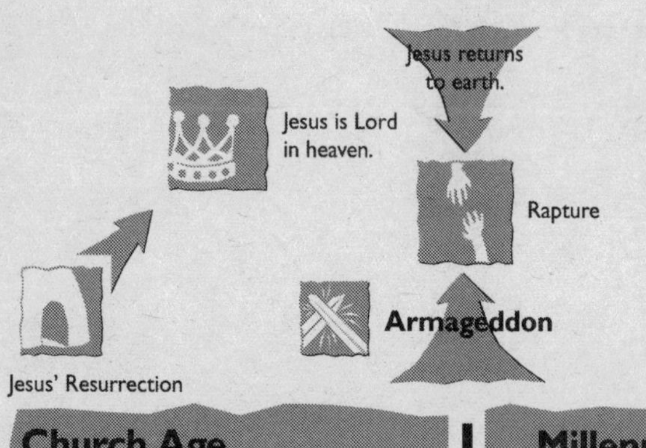

Church Age

- Church spreads the Good News.
- There will be a period of tribulation toward the end of the church age.

The Millennium

- Jesus physically rules on earth for 1,000 years.

Christ's Second Coming

- Christ defeats the antichrist at Armageddon.
- Believers meet Christ in midair.
- Believers descend to earth to reign with Jesus in the millennial kingdom.
- Satan is thrown in the bottomless pit.

Historic Premillennial View

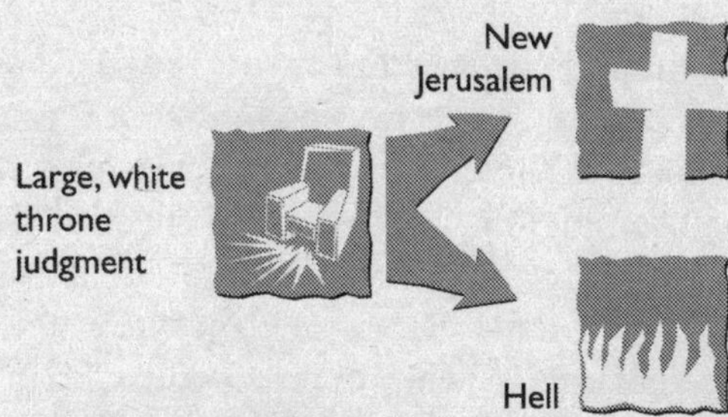

Great Rebellion

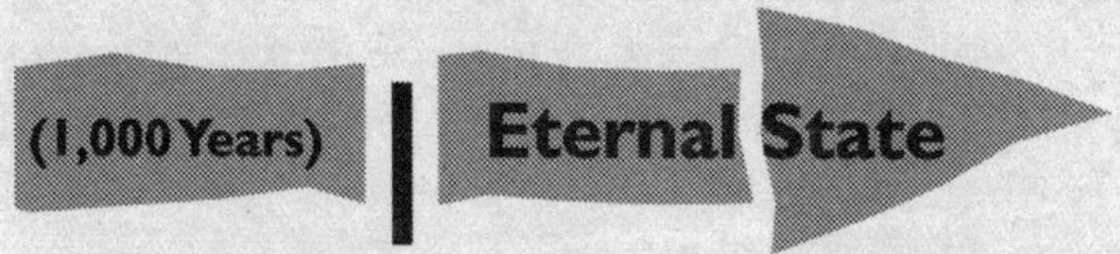

End of the Millennium

- At the end of the millennium, Satan is released.
- Jesus defeats the army Satan has gathered.
- All the dead are raised to face judgment.

Eternity

- Believers go to the New Jerusalem.
- Unbelievers go to hell.

Day 27

AMILLENNIAL VIEW

Matthew 24:31; Revelation 7:13–14

Amillennialists expect the battle between good and evil to climax in a period of intense persecution of Christians at the end of the age, just prior to Jesus' second coming. They believe the Tribulation isn't confined simply to the future, but is present in this age as well. The Tribulation occurs anywhere the Good News message is being opposed and Christians are being persecuted. Amillennialists point out that scripture doesn't state that the Tribulation is confined to Israel (Revelation 7:13–14). They believe all of God's people will be persecuted. When Christ returns bringing judgment on evil, he will gather believers from every direction under the sky (Matthew 24:31).

Need to Know

- It is a powerful image. . .to wash robes in blood and see them turn white and clean. That is the picture of redemption and the purification of persecution described in Revelation 7. Jesus' blood cleanses our consciences (Hebrews 9:14) and gives us God's approval (Romans 3:21–22).
- John wrote Revelation toward the end of the first century. It was a time of growing unrest and tension between church and state. Rome's rule required worship of the emperor as well as allegiance. Refusal to offer up that worship was cause for intense persecu-

tion. John didn't have to look far to understand what tribulation was all about.

Think About It

- What contemporary persecution are you aware of around the world?
- Why do you think, in our modern age, people are still persecuted for the way they think and believe?

Day 28

POSTMILLENNIALISTS AND THE TRIBULATION

John 15:18; John 16:33; Romans 5:3; Romans 8:17; 1 Thessalonians 1:10

Postmillennialists believe the church itself will usher in the Millennium, and deny the idea of a future tribulation. They believe Jesus' prophecy of the sacrilege placed in the temple has already been fulfilled in Rome's destruction of Jerusalem and its temple in AD 70 (Matthew 24:15–22). They don't believe Jesus' prophecy speaks of a future antichrist.

Although people debate whether Christians will go through a time of terrible suffering, we must be ready to suffer for Jesus' sake. Jesus himself warned his disciples that they would experience all types of difficulties and hardships in this world (John 15:18–20; 16:33). As followers of Christ, we can expect trials and tribulations in our lives, but God promises that he won't desert us (John 15:18; 17:15; Romans 8:17; 1 Thessalonians 1:10). If our hope and trust is in Christ, we don't have to fear the future—no matter what it holds.

Need to Know

- Rome ruled Palestine from around AD 44 through AD 66. The Jews rebelled against Roman rule for four years until AD 70, when Jerusalem was attacked by the armies of Emperor Titus and her people butchered. The temple, just finally completed by Herod a few years earlier, was destroyed.
- The English word for "tribulation" comes from the Latin word *tribulum*, "a threshing sledge," giving the idea of tightness, a pressing together. The majority of biblical references to tribulation are to the sufferings of God's people.

Think About It

- How would it change your view of the end times to believe that many of the events John described had already taken place in the first century?
- In what ways do you believe the Christians of your current culture are unprepared for suffering?

Day 29

THE JUDGMENT OF GOD

Nahum 1:3; 2 Peter 3:9

In his grace and goodness, God has been withholding his judgment for thousands of years. The apostle Peter describes it this way: "The Lord is not slack concerning his promise, as some men count slackness; but is longsuffering to us-ward, not willing that any should perish, but that all should come to repentance" (2 Peter 3:9). God has been more than fair with humankind.

When the time comes for God's holy judgment, though, his punishment will be swift and complete. We need to look no further than the book of Revelation for evidence of that. Nahum, an Old Testament prophet, offers an apt description of God: "The LORD is slow to anger, and great in power, and will not at all acquit the wicked" (Nahum 1:3).

Need to Know

- Nahum was the prophet who predicted the downfall of Nineveh and the nation for which it was the capital, Assyria. This was the same Nineveh that Jonah had been called to preach to years before.
- God's judgment and humanity's accountability to him has been a part of the story since Adam and Eve disobeyed God in the Garden of Eden. Part of what makes the end-times judgment of God seem so much harsher is the finality of it. The same judgment

of sin and death was introduced in Eden, but the actuality of that judgment will be bitter.

Think About It

- In what ways do you feel accountable to God on a daily basis?
- How does your hope in Christ affect how you think of God's final judgment?

Day 30

THE TRADITIONAL VIEW

Daniel 9:24; Mark 1:10–11; Luke 4:18; Hebrews 1:1–3

Many Christians believe that Daniel's seventy weeks were fulfilled in Jesus' first coming, and that there are no future events in Daniel 9. They believe Jesus fulfilled all six purposes of Daniel's seventy weeks (Daniel 9:24). They contend that Christ's death paid the penalty for our sin, bringing an "end of sins," rebellion, and guilt (Hebrews 9:26; 10:12–14). Moreover, Jesus established our "everlasting righteousness" by his death on the cross (Romans 3:21–22; 5:17–18). They suggest that "sealing the vision and prophecy" refers to the coming of Christ, the final Prophet (Acts 3:22; Hebrew 1:1–3). They interpret the sixth purpose, "anoint the Most Holy," as predicting the Holy Spirit's anointing of Jesus at his baptism (Mark 1:10–11; Luke 4:18).

Need to Know

- To review, in response to Daniel's prayer about Jerusalem, God sent the angel Gabriel, with a prophecy about seventy time periods, translated *weeks* by some. The interpretation of this prophecy has become a bedrock of end-times interpretations.
- Before Jesus came, there were prophets of God who spoke God's truth and foretold the future. Most of their prophecies looked forward to the Messiah, who would be sent from God to save his people. After Jesus' life, death, and resurrection, we look back to the story of Jesus to learn how to live. Jesus was the final prophet in that regard.

Think About It

- What would it mean for your view of the end times to believe that Daniel's prophecies were already accomplished in Christ?
- What did Christ's death accomplish in your life?

Day 31

FULFILLED IN CHRIST

Daniel 9:26–27

Though it's unclear from the text whether Jerusalem's destruction and the defilement of the temple (Daniel 9:26–27) belong within Daniel's seventy weeks, the traditional view states that these two events were fulfilled when Titus destroyed the temple in AD 70. So according to the traditionalists, everything Daniel predicted in the seventieth week has already been fulfilled.

These two different ways of interpreting Daniel's seventy weeks (already fulfilled or yet to be fulfilled) are clearly at odds. But at the same time, they both recognize that Daniel's prophecies are fulfilled in Christ—whether he fulfilled them in the past or will fulfill them in the future. In either case, we can look forward to the day when Christ will return and reveal to us exactly how these prophecies foretold his life.

Need to Know

- The book of Daniel is made up of stories from Daniel's life as a Jewish exile in Persia and Daniel's prophetic visions.
- Daniel's visions included four beasts (chapter 7), a ram and a goat (chapter 8), a prayer with an angelic response (chapter 9), and what is considered a vision of the end times (chapters 10–12).

Think About It

- No matter which interpretation of Daniel's seventy weeks is true, how is Jesus your Messiah, your champion, your Savior today?
- In what ways do you find it difficult to deal with someone who has a very different view of the end times than you do?

Day 32

THE FOUR HORSEMEN OF THE APOCALYPSE

Revelation 6:1–8

In Revelation 6, John describes four horsemen as introducing God's judgment on the world. The first rides a white horse; the second, a fiery red horse; the third, a black horse; and the fourth, a pale horse. Each one has a mission related to the Lamb's breaking of the first four seals of judgment (Revelation 6:1–8).

Opening the first seal releases a rider with a bow on a white horse (Revelation 6:2). This is the only rider who doesn't cause some kind of a catastrophe on the earth. He merely rides out to win battles. There is much debate over who or what this horseman represents. Some commentators have suggested this horseman symbolizes the proclamation of the Good News of Christ, while others see him as representing the rise of false Christs. The color of the horse seems to point to the Good News interpretation, for Jesus is closely associated with the color white in Revelation (Revelation 1:14; 7:14; 14:14; 19:11). On the other hand, the fact that this white horse and rider precede three other horsemen who wreak havoc on the earth suggests that the white horseman might represent the rise of false Christs.

Need to Know

- The color white is used throughout scripture to represent purity and holiness. "Though your sins be as scarlet, they shall be as white as snow" (Isaiah 1:18).
- In his discourse on the end times, Jesus talked about false Christs. He warned his followers to be on their guard even against those who could perform miracles (see Mark 13:22–23).

Think About It

- What Christian beliefs are you aware of upon which there are many differing interpretations?
- How do you see Jesus as a victory-winner in your life?

Day 33

AGENTS OF JUDGMENT

Revelation 6:3–8

At the breaking of the second seal, the rider of a red horse is given a large sword to provoke warfare and slaughter on the earth (Revelation 6:3–4).

The third seal unleashes a black horse whose rider holds a scale, symbolizing economic hard times and sorrow (Revelation 6:5–6, 12). A voice declares that the cost for barley and wheat are twelve to fifteen times the normal price, suggesting inflation and famine. But this famine is not extreme since other staples like olive oil and wine are not affected.

The fourth seal unleashes a pale horse, ridden by "Death," who is given power to kill a quarter of the earth's population through war, famine, plagues, and wild animals (Revelation 6:7–8). The horse's pale color suggests fear as well as impending death. "Hell" follows this horse on foot, grimly devouring the dead.

Need to Know

- A sword is used throughout the Bible as a symbol for and tool of war. It was the first weapon of offense mentioned. A sword guarded the Garden of Eden after Adam and Eve were sent away.
- Scales were a symbol of equality and judgment. While used in commerce to weigh goods, they were also mentioned by Ezekiel, Daniel, and others as a way to measure a person's integrity.

Think About It

- What are the images or symbols our culture would choose today to denote war and death?
- What elements of your relationship with God allow you to be free of the fears associated with famine, war, and death?

Day 34

THE MEANING OF THE HORSEMEN

Romans 8:22–24; Revelation 5:4, 8–10

What is the meaning of these horsemen? Why does the Lamb break the seals? To answer these questions, we need to look at the broader context of this vision in Revelation.

The four horsemen are part of a vision that describes the breaking of seven seals on a bound scroll (Revelation 5). Many scholars believe that this scroll represents God's plan for history. Amillennialists interpret the scroll as God's redemptive plan for history, while premillennialists interpret it as God's plan for the final days before Jesus' second coming (Daniel 12:1–4). No wonder John weeps when no one is able to open the scroll (Revelation 5:4). If the scroll remains bound, evil will continue unabated and there will be no future for God's people. But the slain Lamb appears, and the heavenly hosts sing that he is worthy to open the scroll because he has "redeemed us to God by [his] blood" (Revelation 5:9). As a result of Christ's redemption, believers will reign with Christ on earth (Revelation 5:8–10).

Need to Know

- Jesus' role as the Lamb hearkens back to the earliest Jewish traditions of sacrificial lambs, most specifically the Passover Lamb. In Egypt, the blood of an innocent lamb was placed on the doorposts of Hebrew homes, and thus the angel of death was kept from taking the firstborn of the household (Exodus 12:21–23).

- When the Lamb, Jesus, opens the scroll, even though the immediate consequence is havoc, it is a fulfillment of the promise woven throughout the New Testament of our redemption and adoption into God's family (Romans 8:22–24).

Think About It

- What does it mean to you that you will "reign on the earth" with Christ?
- Jesus gave his life so that you could be adopted as a child of God. In what ways do you express your gratitude for that?

Day 35

THE SCROLL AND ITS SEVEN SEALS

Matthew 24:4–8; Mark 13:5–8; Luke 21:8–9

What is the relationship between the seals and the content of the scroll (see Revelation 6)? To open an ancient scroll, a person had to break every wax seal. Some commentators believe that the seals described in Revelation are predicting what will occur before the scroll is opened—that is, before the end of the world.

Note the striking similarities between Jesus' description of the "beginning pains" of the end times and the breaking of these four seals. Jesus declared that false Christs, wars, famines, plagues, and persecutions would precede his Second Coming (Matthew 24:4–8; Mark 13:5–13; Luke 21:8–19), just as is described in the vision of the seals in Revelation.

Need to Know

- Just like safety seals appear today on foods and medicines ("Do not open if seal is broken") or documents that are notarized, ancient scrolls were sealed with wax or clay. The seals were often stamped with the sender's seal, usually kept as a ring on his finger or around his neck. These ancient seals functioned in the same way as their modern counterparts, both for protection and validation of the contents.
- In the ancient world, a pestilence (a contagious epidemic disease) was seen as an act of judgment from God rather than a natural phenomenon or random event.

Think About It

- How do you make sense of God's plan when everything is going wrong all around?
- What recent headlines seem to be a part of the "beginning of sorrows" that Jesus described in Mark?

Day 36

THE MEANING OF THE BREAKING OF THE SEALS

Revelation 17:14

Why does Christ break the scroll's seals and permit such devastation? Keep in mind that the Revelation was written for Christians who were being persecuted. In breaking these seals, Christ isn't ordering devastation and destruction. Such evil already exists in this world. Rather, the description of Christ breaking the seals demonstrates his lordship over human history—even the evil that occurs in history. This vision assures believers that despite present appearances, Christ is unfolding a future in which he will triumph over every enemy (Revelation 17:14). Believers can have this confidence because Jesus Christ reigns.

Need to Know

- Persecution for first-century Christianity began almost as soon as the movement was recognized. Jesus' life was filled with persecution. After his ascension back to heaven, his followers were persecuted by the Jews for perpetuating the gospel story. When the Christians then refused to worship Caesar, they became enemies of the state.
- From the first conflict between God and Adam and Eve, and between Cain and Abel, evil has been a part of our world. Many words are used to denote evil in biblical texts, most of them containing some

element of destruction, disaster, calamity, wickedness, and downfall.

Think About It

- What specific enemies or evils of this world do you look forward to Jesus triumphing over?
- In the midst of the troubles in the world and the coming greater troubles, what signs of God's redemption and sovereignty do you see?

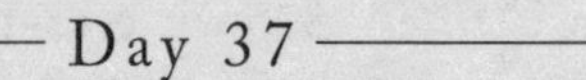

Day 37

THE RAPTURE

Matthew 24:37–44; 1 Thessalonians 4:16–18

"Two women shall be grinding at the mill; the one shall be taken, and the other left" (Matthew 24:41). Jesus' description of the day he returns has sparked the imaginations of many. What would it be like if half of a town's population suddenly disappeared? Would cars spin out of control, as those bumper stickers suggest: "WARNING: In case of rapture this vehicle will be unattended"?

The term *rapture*, meaning "to seize" or "to carry away," is an integral part of Paul's description of Christ's return. At this event, believers are literally pulled up to meet Christ in the air (1 Thessalonians 4:16–18). While most Christians believe in a future rapture event, there are obviously a variety of views regarding its nature and timing.

Need to Know

- The Rapture will be, among other things, a mass resurrection. Paul said, "the dead in Christ shall rise first." There were a few resurrections in Scripture before the resurrection of Jesus. Through God's power, the prophet Elisha raised a boy from the dead (2 Kings 4). Jesus raised people from the dead, perhaps the most famous being Lazarus: "Lazarus, come out!" (John 11 CEV).
- From the beginning, death has been the enemy. Eve's conversation with the serpent was about death ("Ye shall not surely die. . . ."). Jesus' resurrection was a victory over death. While the end times, including the Rapture, can be mysterious and even scary, it is about life over death.

Think About It

- What do you or others you know fear about the Rapture?
- If you were given the job of fashioning a new end-times bumper sticker, what would it say?

—— Day 38 ——

TWO WITNESSES IN JERUSALEM

Revelation 11:3–13

In the midst of the Tribulation, a period of unprecedented evil and persecution, two voices will shout out a message of hope. Revelation 11:3–13 tells us that two witnesses will preach God's word in Jerusalem and throughout the world for 1,260 days. Anyone who tries to harm these messengers during that time will be destroyed. These two witnesses for God will possess supernatural powers—the ability to stop rain from falling, to turn water into blood, and to cause plagues.

After three and a half years, the witnesses will be killed by the beast, the antichrist. For three and a half days, their dead bodies will lie in the street for the whole world to see—perhaps this spectacle will be viewed via satellite television. In any case, the whole world will celebrate because they won't have to listen to the two witnesses anymore. The celebration will be short-lived, though. After their bodies have been left in the streets for three and a half days, the witnesses will be brought back to life and will ascend to heaven. Their resurrection will frighten people and cause many to turn to Christ.

Need to Know

- There has been much speculation as to the identity of the two witnesses. Some believe that they will be Enoch and Elijah, both Old Testament ancients who were taken to heaven without dying. Others believe they will be Moses and Elijah, who did similar miracles to those described in Revelation 11. Still others believe the two witnesses are just symbols of the church.
- John wrote that the witnesses would be dressed in sackcloth. This was a symbol of mourning. Sackcloth

was usually coarse and dark. It was often worn by prophets who grieved over the sins of their people or warned them of coming doom.

Think About It

- What grieves you most about the current state of the church?
- If you were one of the last witnesses on earth, what would you say?

Day 39

FALSE PROPHETS

Matthew 24:24; Revelation 13:11–17

"For there shall arise false Christs, and false prophets." Jesus' words in Matthew 24:24 serve as a warning to believers of every generation. They will be especially applicable to the people living during the end times. Revelation 13:11–17 describes a "second beast," one who will persuade the world to follow the first beast, the antichrist (Revelation 13:1–10). This second beast, also known as the false prophet, will use supernatural tricks and miracles—such as calling down fire from heaven and bringing a statue to life—to deceive people into worshiping the antichrist. Those who don't evaluate this false prophet's teaching against the truth of God's Word, those who don't have the courage to reject this prophet, will be caught under his spell.

Need to Know

- Some believe that this second beast is an actual individual, but others believe it will be a movement or power that takes worldwide control.
- This second beast completes what some people refer to as the "unholy trinity," made up of Satan, the antichrist, and the prophet—counterparts to the Father, Son, and Holy Spirit.

Think About It

- What vulnerabilities do you see around you that sets up our society to be easily deceived by false prophets?
- What can you do today to ensure that you know the truth well enough not to be deceived by false teachers?

Day 40

POSTMILLENNIAL VIEW

Matthew 28:18–20; Hebrews 4:12; Revelation 1:16

Postmillennialists believe that Christ is currently leading his church to victory over all its enemies through the renewing power of God's Word (Matthew 28:18–20). Evangelists and Christians who try to spread the Good News of Christ will always face obstacles. Yet postmillennialists don't believe that wickedness and persecution will significantly increase as the world draws to a close.

Postmillennialists insist that the church today is transforming society gradually in the same way that yeast permeates bread (Matthew 13:33). They believe Armageddon represents Christ's victory over evil forces throughout church history. They point out that scripture describes the Lamb as conquering with the sword of his mouth—in other words, Jesus conquers his enemies spiritually, through the preaching of God's Word (Hebrews 4:12; Revelation 19:11–21). In this way, God will triumph over all opposition and establish a period of spiritual prosperity: the millennial kingdom.

Need to Know

- The Psalms as well as many New Testament verses tell about the benefits of God's Word. The scriptures equip us, renew us, restore us, feed us, and more.
- At the beginning of Revelation, John gave messages to seven churches. The image he described there of Jesus, the Son of man, included a two-edged sword coming out of his mouth (Revelation 1:16). This image fits perfectly with the description in Hebrews 4:12 of God's word being "sharper than any twoedged sword."

Think About It

- How has God transformed you through his Word?
- How do you see the world becoming a better place (or having the potential of it) through God's Word?

TIMELINE FOR THE

Jesus is currently conquering his enemies. *(Rev. 19:11)*

Jesus' Resurrection

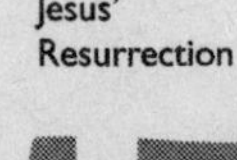

AD 70— Jerusalem Destroyed

Church Age

- Church gradually brings about the millennium by preaching the Good News.
- Prophecies concerning the tribulation were fulfilled in AD 70, when the Romans destroyed Jerusalem. No future tribulation.

Bottomless Pit

Satan is thrown in the bottomless pit at the end of the Church Age.

The Millennium

- Jesus reigns during the millennium in a spiritual sense.
- The whole world worships Jesus.
- The culture becomes "Christian."
- No war.

Postmillennial View

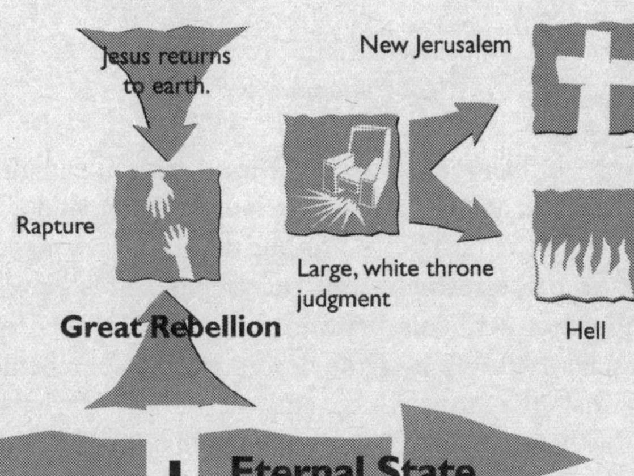

Jesus' Second Coming

- Jesus returns to defeat Satan's Great Rebellion.
- Believers meet Jesus in midair.
- All are raised from the dead to be judged by Christ.

Eternity

- Believers go to the New Jerusalem.
- Unbelievers go to hell.

Day 41

AMILLENNIAL AND HISTORIC PREMILLENNIAL VIEW

1 Corinthians 10:13; 1 Thessalonians 5:9; 2 Thessalonians 2:3–12

Both amillennialists and historic premillennialists believe evil and destruction will increase tremendously in the last days. They point out that Jesus predicted a future of persecution and catastrophe. This time of tribulation will culminate in the antichrist, who will proclaim himself as a god, lead a worldwide rebellion against the true God, and persecute Christians (Matthew 24:15–22; 2 Thessalonians 2:3–12). Both these views insist that Christians will be present on earth during this awful period of tribulation since scripture never promises their escape. However, God *does* promise spiritual protection for his people during times of persecution (1 Corinthians 10:13; 1 Thessalonians 1:10; 5:9).

Both amillennialists and historic premillennialists believe that the vision of Armageddon in Revelation figuratively portrays the final rebellion against God. As a result, they place more attention on the Second Coming than on the actual battle itself.

Need to Know

- There are many parts of the Bible over which scholars and theologians disagree about whether the narrative is symbolic or whether the events actually did (or will) occur. Still, there are many applications and encouragements to be found in these very scriptures no matter which way a person leans on the issue.
- Remember that the antichrist is one of the three in the unholy trinity of Satan, the antichrist, and the false prophet.

Think About It

- If Christians do remain on earth through the Tribulation, how can you and others be ready?
- What are you facing in this season of life that will prepare you for tribulations and persecutions?

Day 42

DISPENSATIONAL PREMILLENNIAL VIEW

Daniel 7:20–27; Revelation 16:16; Revelation 19:19–21

Dispensational premillennialists have developed a detailed scenario for what they see as the battle of Armageddon. They believe the future tribulation will not begin until after the Rapture—that time when all believers, living and dead, meet the Lord in midair and return to heaven with him. Dispensationalists believe that God will use the Tribulation to bring Israel back to himself.

During the Tribulation, the antichrist emerges as the leader of the restored Roman Empire. At first the antichrist befriends Israel. But after three and a half years, he begins a horrible persecution of the Jews (Daniel 7:8, 20–27; 9:24–27; Matthew 24:15–22). Because of this, Israel begins to return to God. At the height of his persecution of God's people, the antichrist's own worldwide power base begins to crumble. The battle of Armageddon begins when the king of the north and the king of the south converge on Israel to attack the antichrist and his troops. After these armies are defeated, the kings of the east invade Israel, resulting in the final campaign of Armageddon (Revelation 16:16). Then at the last hour, Christ miraculously and decisively intervenes in this horrific battle. At the battlefield of Armageddon, he demonstrates his power and destroys all remaining foes (Revelation 19:19–21).

Need to Know

- The kings involved in Armageddon (and pre-Armageddon) are probably the national leaders who join in alliance with the antichrist.
- It is after Christ's victory at Armageddon that the lake of fire comes into play. It is the final destination of all that is evil.

Think About It

- What typifies evil in your culture?
- What does Christ's definitive victory over all evil offer you today as you battle with evil in your world?

Timeline for the

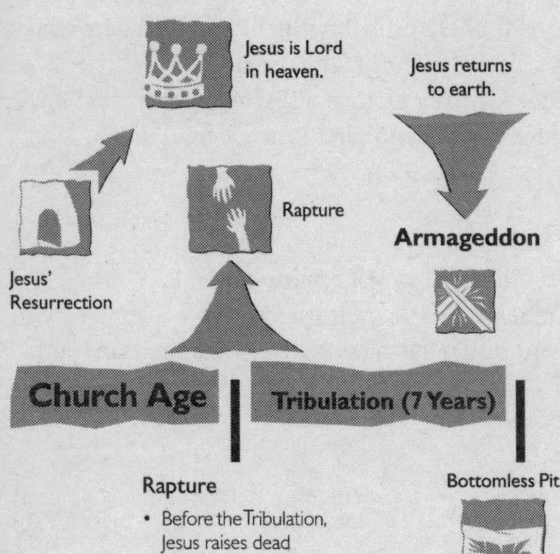

Rapture

- Before the Tribulation, Jesus raises dead believers and takes living believers to heaven.
- Believers are judged.

Christ's Second Coming

- Christ defeats the antichrist at Armageddon.
- Christ throws Satan in the bottomless pit.
- Tribulation martyrs are raised from the dead.

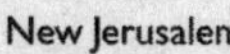

Large, white throne judgment

Hell

Millennium (1,000 Years)

Eternal State

The Millennium

- Jesus physically rules on earth for 1,000 years.

End of the Millennium

- Unbelievers are raised from the dead to be judged.

Eternity

- Believers go to the New Jerusalem.
- Unbelievers go to hell.

Day 43

EVIL WILL BE CONQUERED

Matthew 12:25–29; Revelation 1:18; Revelation 21:4

While interpretations of the closing events of the Tribulation and of Armageddon differ sharply, all believers agree that Jesus has already defeated both Satan and death itself (Matthew 12:25–29; Revelation 1:18). Ultimately, evil won't prevail. One way or another, Christ will decisively demonstrate his power over Satan and his evil forces. So we don't have to concentrate on the hardships of the Tribulation or the suffering at Armageddon; we can look forward to a new age in which Christ "will wipe away all tears" from our eyes and evil will be no more (Revelation 21:4).

Need to Know

- Christ's ultimate victory over evil was first foretold by God to the serpent that deceived Eve. He promised that one would come that would bruise that serpent's head (Genesis 3:15). It is at the end of Armageddon that Jesus makes good on that promise.
- The force of evil has always been a force of destruction. God is the source of life and God's path leads to life. Jesus himself claimed to be the way, the truth, and the life. A victory over evil is victory over death itself.

Think About It

- Who do you see as the victims of evil in the world around you?
- What do you see as your role in the battle against evil?

Day 44

SATAN'S WAR WITH GOD

Isaiah 14:13–14; Jude 1:6; Revelation 12:9

According to Genesis 1–2, God created human beings for relationship with himself and placed them in a paradise called the Garden of Eden. Satan, disguised as a serpent, disrupted God's plan by leading Adam and Eve into disobedience (Genesis 3:13–15; Revelation 12:9). So people are enslaved to a power greater than they are—namely, Satan, the prince of evil (Matthew 12:22–32; 1 John 5:19).

Satan was originally an angel created for God's glory. But Satan arrogantly rebelled, desiring to be like God, and was thrown from heaven (Jude 1:6). Satan's flamboyant pride is reflected in the words of the prophets Ezekiel and Isaiah to the kings of Babylon: "Thus saith the Lord God; Thou sealest up the sum, full of wisdom, and perfect in beauty. . . . Thine heart was lifted up because of thy beauty, thou hast corrupted thy wisdom by reason of thy brightness: I will cast thee to the ground" (Ezekiel 28:12, 17). "For thou hast said in thine heart, I will ascend into heaven, I will exalt my throne above the stars of God: I will sit also upon the mount of the congregation, in the sides of the north: I will ascend above the heights of the clouds; I will be like the most High" (Isaiah 14:13–14).

Need to Know

- The name *Satan* comes from a Hebrew word that means "accuser" (see Revelation 12:10). In the Old Testament Satan is portrayed as the one who tries to sit as judge on God. The name *Devil* is a Greek translation of the same name.
- In John's Gospel he referred to Satan (quoting Jesus) as the "prince of this world" (John 12:31). While it is true that Satan has some dominion over our world, God is still sovereign and will overcome in the end.

Think About It

- Do you see the will of Satan in any part of the world around you?
- What are your greatest weapons to stand against Satan and his forces?

Day 45

SATAN'S WICKED WORK

John 8:44; Revelation 13:4–8

When Adam and Eve rebelled, they were hoping they could become like God and free themselves from God. But in reality, they allowed the entire human race to be enslaved to Satan. Scripture repeatedly describes Satan as the "prince" or "god of this world" (John 14:30; 2 Corinthians 4:4). His rule pervades every area of this world. Oppressive and unjust political structures reveal Satan's reign (Revelation 12:13; 13:4–8; 18:1–20). Even the curse of death and sickness that God pronounced in Eden reflects Satan's work (Mark 5:1–15; John 8:44).

Need to Know

- Satan's claim to Eve in the Garden was that God had lied to her. The serpent said that Eve wouldn't die if she ate the fruit, as God had said. Instead, she would become like God. Satan's role from the beginning was to undermine the truth of who God is and what he says.
- Jesus was once accused of working through the power of Satan. It was in response to that accusation that Jesus gave an often-quoted reply: a "house divided against itself shall not stand" (Matthew 12:25). This reply pointed out to his accusers their lack of logic. The very miracle Jesus had performed

was the casting out of demons. Why would he have done that under the power of Satan?

Think About It

- Can you spot areas in your life where God's truth has been undermined?
- How would you define the work of Satan in this modern world?

Day 46

SATAN'S STRUGGLE WITH GOD

Genesis 3:15; Luke 10:18–19; John 12:31–33

After Adam and Eve's sin in the Garden of Eden, God promised that he would destroy Satan and his demons and reestablish his own kingdom. Speaking to the serpent, God said, "And I will put enmity between thee and the woman, and between thy seed and her seed; it shall bruise thy head, and thou shalt bruise his heel" (Genesis 3:15). The offspring who ultimately crushes Satan's head is God's promised Messiah, Jesus Christ.

When Jesus demonstrated his power over Satan's realm through his miracles and exorcisms, he was, in a sense, binding the "strong man" of this world (Matthew 12:28–29). Hearing of his disciples' success on their first mission to spread his word, Jesus said, "I beheld Satan as lightning fall from heaven. Behold, I give unto you power. . .over all the power of the enemy" (Luke 10:18–19).

Jesus' sacrificial death on the cross and his resurrection sealed his victory over Satan. Christ disarmed the evil powers and authorities (Colossians 2:15; John 12:31; 16:11).

Need to Know

- Christ's death on the cross appeared to be a defeat, yet it was the moment of greatest victory. It was the connecting point between God's promise in the Garden and Jesus' eventual victory at Armageddon.
- During Jesus' time on earth, Satan's demons recognized him as the Son of God long before Jesus' fellow Israelites did. The demons recognized Jesus' authority. When he was casting the demons out of Legion, they spoke up to negotiate their transfer into the swine rather than being sent away (Mark 5:1–13).

Think About It

- What does it mean to you that Jesus has given Christians authority over Satan?
- What fears, if any, do you have regarding Satan's power and influence?

Day 47

SATAN'S FINAL BATTLE

James 4:7; 1 Peter 5:8–10; Revelation 12:7–9

Revelation 12:7–9 describes a war in heaven between Satan and the archangel Michael. After Satan is defeated and ejected from heaven, his battle against God's people becomes even more ruthless (Revelation 12:12). Now in his death throes, Satan "walketh about, seeking whom he may devour" (1 Peter 5:8). Members of the first-century church understood Satan's intentions. They warned one another to resist evil (James 4:7) and even expected to have "tribulation" (Acts 14:22; John 16:33). Believers have only experienced the first stage of Christ's victory over Satan. While Satan's final destruction is certain, we are presently waiting for Christ to "bruise Satan" and to end all evil (Romans 16:20).

Our only hope against Satan is Jesus Christ. Christ alone is more powerful than Satan. His grace, brought to us by the Holy Spirit, can put Satan on the run (Romans 8:26; 1 Peter 5:8–10). Guard yourself against Satan by keeping your eyes fixed on Jesus!

Need to Know

- Peter's description of Satan attacking as a lion is an apt one. In the wild, lions often attack the weak, sick, or struggling—those who will fall most easily.
- Paul also warned against the attacks of Satan. One of his most famous warnings is a preamble to the description of the armor of God (Ephesians 6:12).

Think About It

- What will be my most vulnerable place today, the place where evil could influence me?
- How can I, in a practical way, trust in God's power over Satan's evil?

Day 48

BABYLON: THE NOTORIOUS PROSTITUTE

Jeremiah 51:47–49; Revelation 18:10–14

Babylon is the name given to the satanically influenced civilization that figures prominently in end-times events. Babylon is the wellspring of ungodly religion, government, and economics. From the wickedness of Babylon, the most evil ruler the world has ever known, the beast (antichrist), will emerge. In Revelation 17, an angel calls Babylon a notorious prostitute. She will tempt the rulers of every nation to blaspheme God and commit sexual sins. The beast will use Babylon's false religion to gain power. Once the beast is established, he will turn against Babylon and create his own religious system (Revelation 17:16–17). The beast will utterly demolish Babylon and all its luxuries (Revelation 18), and the merchants of the world will weep over this fallen civilization.

Need to Know

- Ancient Babylon is often mentioned in Old Testament prophecies. It was Babylon that finally overtook Judah (what remained of the nation of Israel) and carried the Jews into exile (Jeremiah 51:47–49; 2 Kings 25:21).
- From the time of ancient Israel, the spiritual unfaithfulness of the people was described in terms of adultery. That is why Babylon is described as a prostitute; the false religions of Babylon seduced God's people away.

Think About It

- What "Babylons" do you sense around you—modern influences that deliberately try to undermine the Christian faith?
- What are your own personal "Babylons" that pull and tear at your spirituality?

Day 49

THE GREAT RED DRAGON

Revelation 20:1–3, 7–10

"Great red dragon" is one of John's favorite nicknames for Satan. In Revelation 12, the apostle witnesses a war in heaven between God's angels led by Michael, and the forces of evil led by the red dragon, or serpent. After losing the battle, Satan and his angels will be thrown out of heaven to the earth. Recognizing that his time on earth is short, the serpent will use the beast (antichrist) to wage war against God's people (Revelation 13:1–2). When Jesus returns, the serpent will be overpowered and chained in the bottomless pit for "a thousand years" (Revelation 20:2). At the end of that time, he will be released briefly and allowed to wreak havoc by deceiving anyone he can into joining him in a war against God. The serpent's eternal fate will be sealed when he is thrown into the fiery lake of sulfur forever (Revelation 20:7–10).

Need to Know

- In scripture there are often parallels between good and evil. Here Satan is referred to as a great red dragon and serpent. Moses once used a bronze serpent sculpture on a pole to grant healing to his people suffering from poisonous snakebites. In the New Testament that snake statue was referred to as a symbol of Christ's crucifixion and its healing power. Symbols can mean different things in different situations.

- The bottomless pit, the abyss, is the exact opposite of heaven. It is the seat of wickedness and destruction. It is the source of evil, just as heaven is the source of God's goodness.

Think About It

- What are the ways in which you think "red serpent" is an apt description of Satan as you have observed his work in your lifetime?
- In what ways do you now see Satan fighting against God's people?

Day 50

THE RELEASE OF THE DEMONS

Revelation 12:9; Revelation 16:10–14

Demons have always made effective villains and monsters in our culture. Their supernatural abilities and evil nature have provided images and tales for countless novels, television shows, and movies. But how accurate are these portrayals? Are demons really dangerous, frightening beings?

Demons are fallen angels (Revelation 12:9). They are sinful spiritual beings who recognize Satan as their leader (Matthew 25:41; Luke 11:15). The book of Revelation highlights three evil powers who oppose God's people in the end times: Satan, in the guise of a serpent (Revelation 12:9); the beast, better known as the antichrist (Revelation 13:1–10); and the false prophet (Revelation 13:11; 16:13). Demons serve as agents of this evil trinity. They seduce people, establish the notorious kingdom of Babylon, and lead a worldwide offensive against God's people (Revelation 16:1–14).

Need to Know

- Jesus was accused of doing his work through the power of Beelzebub, the chief of demons. *Beelzebub*, literally meaning "lord of the flies," was another name for Satan.
- The English word for *demon* is derived from a Greek word that means "deity," in this case false deities. There is no specific Hebrew word for demon, but there are Old Testament references to evil spirits.

Think About It

- What is the most effective portrayal of a demon you've witnessed in modern culture?
- In what ways do you think our culture either trivializes or magnifies the work of Satan and his demons?

Day 51

DEMONIC DECEPTION

Ephesians 6:12; Revelation 13:4–15

Revelation vividly illustrates Satan's tendency for disguising himself as an angel of light. Notice how the antichrist gains the world's allegiance through an amazing spectacle. Imitating Christ's resurrection from the dead, the antichrist recovers after receiving a fatal wound (Revelation 13:3). But the false prophet's impersonation of Christ is even more ingenious. Like Christ, the false prophet performs astonishing miracles, including bringing a statue to life (Revelation 13:14–15). The demons also, with their dazzling miracles, deceive people and entrap the entire world (Revelation 16:1–14).

To prevent demonic miracles from leading people astray, the book of Revelation offers some insight on identifying demonic work. Babylon, described as the dwelling place of demons, is marked by three specific sins: idolatry, self-absorption, and self-sufficiency (Revelation 18:2–3, 7). Here, the distinction between what is godly and what is demonic becomes most obvious. Babylon represents the perversion of godly virtues: idolatry rather than worship of God, materialism rather than dependence on God, conceited thoughts of invincibility rather than the humility of the Lamb.

The book of Revelation clearly states that while demons may imitate God's power, they pervert his truth and character. This explains why the false prophet looks "like a lamb," but talks "as a dragon" (Revelation 13:11).

Need to Know

- A good example of demonic work can be seen in a prayer of Daniel. When the angel Michael arrived with the answer to Daniel's prayer, he claimed that a demon, "the prince of the kingdom of Persia," had hindered him on his journey (Daniel 10:10–13).
- According to Ephesians 6:12 there may be a hierarchy of demonic society: principalities, powers, rulers of the darkness of this world, spiritual wickedness in high places.

Think About It

- What elements of our society do you see as foundational weaknesses that will allow people to be deceived by false deities?
- From your experience, what are Satan's most effective disguises?

Day 52

DEMONIC PERSECUTION

Revelation 12:1–9; Revelation 17:14

Vicious demonic attacks intensify after Michael, the archangel, ejects Satan from heaven (Revelation 12:7–9). The defeated Satan, knowing that his time is short, does everything in his power to destroy God's people (Revelation 12:12–17). It's important to remember, though, that the Lamb (Jesus) has already conquered these evil powers at the Cross, and he will one day demonstrate his power over them. Even as demonic forces viciously attack God's people, Revelation assures us that these evil powers have no future. They are already defeated! Their warfare against God is useless because Christ has already defeated them at the cross (Revelation 5:5; 12:1–11; 17:14; 19:1–21). At the final judgment, the demons will meet their ultimate destiny: the lake of fire and brimstone (Matthew 25:41; Revelation 20:10).

Need to Know

- The word for *fire* in the lake of fire is sometimes translated "burning sulphur." This place is called the second death because it is a final separation from God.
- The residents of the lake of fire will include the beast, the false prophet, Satan, death and hell and all those whose names are not found in the Book of Life.

Think About It

- How would you describe the kind of suffering that is caused by separation from God?
- What kind of alternate image would you paint of a place that was ultimate destruction?

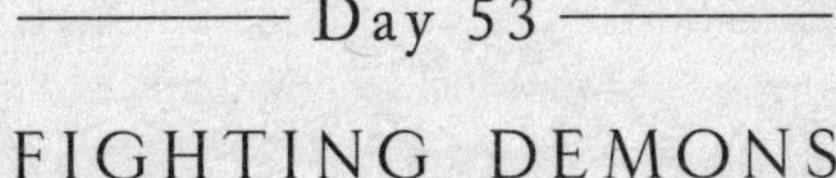

FIGHTING DEMONS

Ephesians 6:13–17; Revelation 12:10–12

Revelation's marvelous visions of the conquering Christ should remind us that God will ultimately bring evil to an end (Revelation 13:10). During the Tribulation, believers must remain focused on Jesus and only follow him. Demons can assume a beguiling appearance that easily leads people astray, so Christians must remain steeped in the Word of God and obey Jesus (Ephesians 6:10–19; 1 Peter 5:8–9). God's people must not love their lives "unto the death" (Revelation 12:11). Believers know that demons are, in fact, doomed. Christ has defeated Satan. The demons are already conquered!

Need to Know

- For spiritual battle, Ephesians 6 tells us that God has given both defensive weapons (shield of faith, helmet of salvation) and offensive weapons (sword of the Spirit, the Word of God).

- Revelation 12:10–12 is a hymn of sorts. It is a celebration of God's victory over Satan. That victory was won when God expelled Satan from heaven. It was won with the death of Christ and validated through the martyrs of the faith. That victory will be finalized in the events described in Revelation.

Think About It

- If the demons are already doomed, then why do Christians sometimes feel so powerless against them?
- How will the world be different when evil is brought to an end?

Day 54

WHO IS THE ANTICHRIST?

2 Thessalonians 2:3; Revelation 13:1–3

Throughout history, many world leaders have been suggested as being the antichrist by concerned, but ultimately misguided, Christians. The glimpses we get of the antichrist in scripture are veiled by mysterious imagery—a seven-headed monster with horns and blasphemous names inscribed in each one of its foreheads (Revelation 13:1–3). Though the Bible doesn't identify the antichrist by name, it does offer some intriguing descriptions of him. The apostle Paul calls him "the man of sin" (2 Thessalonians 2:3). Revelation describes him as "the beast" who emerges from the bottomless pit (Revelation 11:7). His entrance on the world stage will involve an astonishing spectacle: he will recover from a fatal wound (Revelation 13:3). We don't know how this event will be accomplished, but it's clear that his power will be derived from Satan himself. That power will extend beyond political and military affairs into the realm of religion. The antichrist will proclaim himself to be a god—and many will believe him.

Need to Know

- The crown of twelve stars worn by the woman in Revelation 12 is a victor's crown. The twelve stars represent the twelve tribes of Israel, though later the woman represents the whole of God's people, Jews and Gentiles alike.
- The child in Revelation 12 that the dragon waited to devour represented the Messiah, Jesus, the long awaited Savior of God's people.

Think About It

- Who are some modern leaders who cross back and forth between the lines of politics and religion?
- How do you think you will recognize the antichrist?

Day 55

HIS ORIGIN AND WORLD DOMINATION

2 Thessalonians 2:3, 7; Revelation 13:7–8

The beast in Revelation doesn't enter the world's stage unexpectedly. He emerges from a great lineage of rebellion (2 Thessalonians 2:3, 7). Similarly, the beast rises from the bottomless pit, the abyss, which represents the satanic underworld (Revelation 11:7). The antichrist is the epitome of the satanic perversions and wickedness that are present in every age.

As a political figure, the antichrist becomes so powerful that opposing him is futile. All nations on earth serve him. Opposition against his rule is brutally suppressed. Only those who are branded with the beast's mark, showing their loyalty to him, will be able to participate in the world's economy (Mark 13:14, 20; Revelation 13:4, 7–8, 16–17).

Need to Know

- In Revelation, the beast is John's symbol for the antichrist while the Lamb is the symbol for Christ. The beast is a counterfeit building his own kingdom as he tries to take the place of Christ.
- The man of sin (or son of perdition) in 2 Thessalonians 2:3 is probably another reference to the antichrist.

Think About It

- How do you think you will be able to differentiate between the antichrist and a power hungry politician?
- What do you believe is the work of the satanic underworld today?

Day 56

THE POWER OF THE ANTICHRIST

Revelation 13:5–8, 14–15

The antichrist blasphemously exalts himself as God and ruthlessly persecutes those who don't worship his image (Daniel 7:21–27; 11:20–39; Mark 13:14, 20; 2 Thessalonians 2:3–4, 9–10). As a result, confessing Jesus as Lord may result in death (Revelation 13:5–8, 15). The antichrist is responsible for unleashing the Tribulation, the most intense period of persecution God's people will ever experience (Mark 13:14, 20).

Using spectacular miracles, the antichrist persuades the world to accept his false teachings (2 Thessalonians 2:9–11). Like Satan, who disguises himself as an angel of light, the beast seduces the world by supposedly imitating Christ's resurrection—when he recovers from a fatal wound (Revelation 13:3, 14).

Need to Know

- Miracles in the Bible were also referred to as *signs* and *wonders*. They signified an act of God, therefore his very presence and power. This is why miracles would give credence to the antichrist's claims to be from God. It would seem God's presence and power had enabled them.
- The antichrist will not be the first to punish those who don't worship the way he chooses. Christians in power through the ages have been guilty of the same persecution, just as they were persecuted by Rome in the first century and in many countries even today.

Think About It

- What consequences do you face now when you publicly confess Jesus as Lord?
- What kinds of consequences do you think would be the hardest for you to face, yet stay true to your convictions?

Day 57

THE GOAL OF THE ANTICHRIST

Daniel 7:26–27; Revelation 7:9–12

The antichrist's aim is principally religious. He exalts himself as nothing less than Jesus' rival. Note the parallels: both are worshiped (Revelation 13:8; 15:2–4); both are killed and come back to life (Revelation 13:3, 8); both have authority over all the nations (Revelation 7:9–12; 13:7); both mark their followers' heads (Revelation 13:16; 14:1). The antichrist not only ravages Christ's followers, he seeks to replace Christ.

Jesus will conquer the antichrist at the great battle of Armageddon. After that, the antichrist and his cohort, the false prophet, will be thrown into the fiery lake (Daniel 7:26–27; 11:36; Revelation 17:14; 19:19–21).

The antichrist reminds us that evil in our world is not simply the compilation of individual human wrongs. There is a "prince of evil" who arrogantly interferes with God's original intent for creation. Satan deceives us and seduces us into his wily schemes, like he has done since the Garden of Eden. Only one person can destroy Satan's power: the Lord Jesus Christ.

Need to Know

- The work of the antichrist will not be new work. Even when the serpent appeared to Eve in the Garden of Eden, he was counterfeiting God when he said, "God told you this, but that's not true. Trust what I tell you instead."

- One of the strongest descriptions of the antichrist outside of the book of Revelation is Paul's letter to the Thessalonians. These Christians had come to believe that they were already in the end times and Jesus' return was so imminent that some had already quit their jobs. Paul assured them that the antichrist would have to come before Christ's return (2 Thessalonians 2:2–12).

Think About It

- What was God's original intent for creation?
- Why do you think the antichrist's efforts are primarily religious rather than political?

Day 58

THE MARK OF THE BEAST

Revelation 13:16–18; Revelation 14:9–12

In the end times, no one will be able to buy or sell anything without the brand of the beast (Revelation 13:16–17). Those who receive the brand of the beast will be readily identifiable. The mark will be stamped prominently on their right hands or foreheads. The mark will be the number 666 (Revelation 13:17–18). No one knows exactly what this number symbolizes.

Those who receive the mark of the beast will benefit economically for a brief time. Their short gain, however, will be quickly offset by the eternal consequences that await them. To receive the brand of the beast is, in essence, to worship the antichrist instead of the one true God. Revelation warns that those who accept the brand of the beast will have to endure God's cup of anger (Revelation 14:9–12; 20:7–15).

Need to Know

- For those who interpret Revelation as a description of events that happened in the first century, the mark of the beast could be a description of Nero, the Roman emperor of the first century who demanded worship, persecuted Christians, and blamed the burning of Rome on them.
- The Bible refers to God marking his own people. In Ezekiel's prophecy a mark is used by God to protect his people from a murderous judgment. These

marks were on the foreheads of the people (Ezekiel 9:4–6). Earlier in Revelation, the 144,000 servants of God were sealed on their foreheads to provide some protection for them for the judgment (Revelation 7:1–4). When the plague of the locusts came, these marked people were protected from death, though not torment (Revelation 9:3–5).

Think About It

- What technologies that you see today could eventually be a part of the process of the taking the mark of the beast?
- What will differentiate the mark of the beast from some of our modern ways of buying and selling, like a check-cashing card?

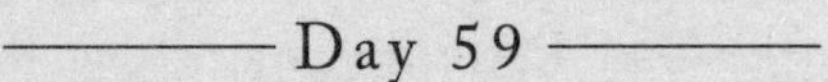

THE BEAST: MAYBE NERO?

Revelation 13:3, 12, 14; Revelation 17:9

Many postmillennialists believe that the prophecies regarding the antichrist have already been fulfilled. Some link the beast in Revelation with the Roman emperor Nero, who committed suicide and who was widely expected to come back to life and reclaim his throne. Those who interpret the antichrist as Nero believe the seven-headed beast symbolizes the evil Roman Empire, because the city of Rome was built on seven hills (Revelation 17:9). Thus, the antichrist was a Roman emperor.

Certainly, there are parallels between the beast and Roman emperors. But this identification of the antichrist with Nero has been seriously challenged. Revelation indicates that the beast itself—the evil empire itself—receives the fatal wound (Revelation 13:3, 12, 14). Nero's suicide hardly endangered the Roman Empire. Today, many doubt whether the antichrist was Nero or any other Roman emperor.

Need to Know

- Nero was the fifth Roman emperor, the last in the family line of Julius Caesar. He ruled from AD 54 until his death in AD 68. While his reign began peacefully, it disintegrated into destruction and death. Nero himself was a suspect in the burning of a large part of Rome in AD 64. He blamed the Christians, thus initiating horrible persecution.
- The name *Caesar* was originally a family name, that of Julius Caesar, who never actually held the title emperor. The name became a title used by emperors such as Augustus and Tiberius, who reigned in the time of Christ.

Think About It

- What principles do you follow in deciding whether scriptures are prophetic of the future or merely descriptions of the past?
- What political leaders in your lifetime most remind you of Nero, famous for destruction more than restoration? How should Christians stand against such leaders?

Day 60

THE BEAST: A WESTERN LEADER?

Revelation 13:1–2; Revelation 17:9–14

Dispensationalists have outlined a detailed scenario for the antichrist. He emerges as the leader of the restored Roman Empire and guarantees the security of Israel (Daniel 7:8, 21–27; 9:24–27; Revelation 17:9–14). After being assassinated, he is restored to life. This only enhances his claims to deity and his goal of world domination. When he exalts himself in the temple at Jerusalem, he reveals his blasphemous and malicious character. His persecution causes Israel to turn to the Messiah. The Tribulation climaxes with military forces converging on Israel to defeat the antichrist.

Some readers question this type of interpretation because it has little biblical evidence to support it. For example, the identification of the beast as the Roman Empire ignores the fact that the beast combines the attributes of all four creatures described in Daniel 7 (Revelation 13:1–2).

Need to Know

- The four creatures, or beasts, in Daniel 7 were a lion with eagle wings, a bear with ribs in its mouth, a leopard with four wings, and a ten-horned beast with a human face. Each of these beasts represented a world power.
- While there is much disagreement here about what

images represent which reality, the truth remains that evil will rise against God and will seem to be winning—but in the end God will triumph.

Think About It

- When you are faced with differing opinions on scripture interpretation, as above, what do you use to make your decisions?
- When you apply the truth of scripture to your life, how do you deal with the unexplainable details you find there?

Day 61

BE WATCHFUL

Matthew 24:4–5; 1 Peter 5:6–11

We should never allow various theories on how prophecies are interpreted to frustrate us. The advocates of all of these theories are following Jesus' command to be watchful (Matthew 24:4–5). They're all looking forward to Jesus' return. Each idea about the identity of the antichrist warns the church to be wary of false prophets—those who seek to lead the church away from Jesus.

Are you being watchful? Remember Peter's warning: "Be sober, be vigilant; because your adversary the devil, as a roaring lion, walketh about, seeking whom he may devour" (1 Peter 5:8).

Need to Know

- Both Paul and Peter reminded their readers that Jesus would come as a thief in the night. In this way, they encouraged the first-century Christians not to assume they knew when Christ would come, but to live in readiness (1 Thessalonians 5:2; 2 Peter 3:10).
- New Testament writers often used the word *asleep* to describe moral indifference. This adds color to the picture of Christ coming as a thief in the night. Those who are *asleep* will not be ready (Mark 13:34–37; Romans 13:10–14).

Think About It

- What do you do to protect yourself from false teaching or falling away from the faith?
- How would you describe your level of readiness for the return of Christ?

Day 62

666

Revelation 13:11–18

"Let him that hath understanding count the number of the beast: for it is the number of a man" (Revelation 13:18). Throughout its history, the church has assigned numerical values to the letters of names in order to identify the beast. Some proposed figures include *Lateinos*, which alludes to the entire Roman Empire; *Neron Kaisar*, under whose direction the church suffered intense persecution; and *Teitan*, for Titus, the Roman Emperor who destroyed Jerusalem in AD 70. The number continues to be linked with various world leaders, institutions, and types of economic transactions.

Many conservative commentators support another proposal. As a representative of apocalyptic literature, the book of Revelation overflows with symbolism. John uses the number *seven* in the book as a symbol of God's perfection. Conversely, the number *six* symbolizes human imperfection. Six is one less than the number seven; three sixes, 666, implies a trinity of imperfection—a perverse parody of the perfection of number seven.

Need to Know

- Numerology is a study of numbers assigning numerical values to the letters of names. Numerology finds meaning in terms of abilities and character

tendencies based on numbers such as date of birth. It is associated with the study of astrology.
- This number of the beast, 666, is possibly one of the most famous numbers from the Bible, though there are many others.

Think About It
- What does the number 666 mean to you?
- Do the symbols of Revelation enlighten you, intrigue you, confuse you? How so?

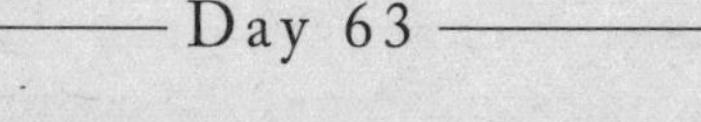

Day 63

GREAT INJUSTICE

Matthew 16:27; Romans 2:6–11

News reports of genocide, sexual abuse, and other unimaginable horrors bombard us every day. The images and stories can harden our hearts. We can even become used to violence and injustice. But God didn't create us that way. Injustice and suffering should always leave us asking: "Who will right these wrongs? When will the wicked be judged? Will justice ever be established?"

God created us accountable to him, the moral Judge of the cosmos. Humanity's rebellion against God is the gravest evil of all and the root of all injustice. God has promised that he will punish all sin (Romans 2:6–11; 12:19). Hell is the horrific and tragic place where the wicked will be paid back for how they have rejected God and mistreated their fellow human beings (Matthew 13:41–42; 16:27).

Sin must be punished. That fact creates a serious human predicament—all have sinned, and so all are under God's judgment (Romans 3:23). The Good News is that God, in the person of Jesus Christ, came to this rebellious world and suffered the punishment for those who have "faith in [Christ's] blood" (Romans 3:25; 2 Corinthians 5:21). Without God's awesome love, people would have no hope.

Need to Know

- God has never let his people off the hook in terms of confronting society. The Old Testament prophets spoke often against poor treatment of the poor and unfortunate.
- New Testament writers often defined Christian faith by how that faith is acted out in the world. While we will never create "heaven on earth," we are not relieved of the responsibility to fight wickedness in our world.

Think About It

- What societal wrongs can you address and do something to change?
- When you observe your community, what evidence do you see that humanity's rebellion against God is the root of all injustice?

Day 64

THE LAKE OF FIRE

Matthew 8:12; Matthew 18:9;
Revelation 20:10, 14–15

At the final judgment, Satan and all of the wicked are cast into the lake of burning sulfur to be "tormented day and night for ever and ever" (Revelation 19:20; 20:10, 14–15). Throughout scripture, fire and burning sulfur are used to portray God's searing holiness as he exacts retribution for evil (Genesis 19:24; Ezekiel 38:22; Hebrews 10:27–31; Revelation 14:9–11). Much speculation has focused on whether these are literal fires. Many biblical scholars, including the Protestant Reformers, noted that a literal fire conflicts with the image of hell as "outer darkness" (Matthew 8:12). Whatever the view, hell is a horrific reality. Jesus' repeated warnings cannot be ignored: "And if thine eye offend thee, pluck it out, and cast it from thee: it is better for thee to enter into life with one eye, rather than. . .be cast into hell fire" (Matthew 18:9).

Need to Know

- Jesus' recommendation to get rid of whatever causes you to lose faith came on the heels of admonition to leaders. He was speaking with his disciples and had just reminded them to come to God as a child. Those who lead have an even greater responsibility to rid their lives of sin.
- The imagery of the lake of fire was probably drawn

from the fires in the Valley of Hinnom. It was this valley outside of Jerusalem that Jesus called Gehenna, the outer darkness.

Think About It

- What would you consider the worst thing about hell?
- What are your greatest temptations to sin?

——— Day 65 ———

FIRE AND DARKNESS

Matthew 25:31–33; Matthew 25:41–46

Although scripture uses images of fiery brimstone and sulfur, destruction, and darkness for hell (Matthew 7:13; 18:8; Jude 13; Revelation 14:10), scripture doesn't describe in excruciating detail the awful fate of hell. Actually, Jesus says more about hell than any other biblical figure. He used the Greek word *gehenna* to describe hell. The word alludes to the valley of Ben Hinnom, where Old Testament Israelites sacrificed their children to false gods and later burned their garbage and refuse (Jeremiah 7:31).

Jesus repeatedly warns that hell is a fate far worse than physical death. Scripture consistently describes hell as a place where one is utterly alone, rejected by one's Creator, and excluded from his loving presence (Matthew 25:12, 41; Luke 13:24–28; 2 Thessalonians 1:8–9).

Need to Know

- "As a shepherd divideth his sheep" (Matthew 25:32), uses the Greek verb *aphorizo* for "divide," meaning to mark off by boundaries or limits, and denotes separation and severing.
- In ancient Canaan, pagan worship of the god Molech was prevalent, along with child sacrifices. It was against God's law for the Israelites to sacrifice children. When the Israelites were tempted to worship Molech, it was with the grave threat of judgment from God.

Think About It

- What do you think people fear most about hell—the physical suffering or the separation from God?
- When you think about separation from God (the essence of hell), what comes to mind?

Day 66

OTHER VIEWS ON HELL

Mark 13:33–37; John 14:6

Some people believe the concept of hell contradicts the idea of Jesus' love for people. *Universalists* believe that everyone, even the wicked, will finally be embraced by God's love.

But universalism hardly agrees with Jesus' own pronouncements. When Jesus offers salvation, he is providing God's unique supernatural intervention (John 14:6). Christians profess that salvation is by grace alone. It reflects God's free decision to save us. Furthermore, Jesus urges us to be ready for his return—to accept his free offer of salvation before it's too late (Matthew 25:13; Mark 13:33–37)—for God's gracious offer of saving love is not an eternal offer (Matthew 25:41). Christ will return in judgment (2 Thessalonians 1:7–10). At that time, it will be too late. Scripture rejects the idea of a second chance after death. Decisions regarding salvation are confined to this life (Hebrews 9:27).

Annihilationists insist that the biblical imagery of a consuming fire implies that the wicked are consumed. Therefore, hell's duration is limited, not everlasting.

Need to Know

- There is a parallel in the Bible between physical death and spiritual death. Adam brought sin into the world. Jesus brought redemption. Adam's legacy is that we all die a physical death. Jesus' legacy is that we are saved from a spiritual death if we choose to be (Romans 5:12; 1 Corinthians 15:22).
- In the Bible salvation comes to us by God's grace, through faith, which is also a gift of God. Yet authentic faith will prompt us to good deeds. There is a balance in which one must be present to validate the other, but we cannot earn our salvation through good deeds (Ephesians 2:8–9; James 2:17).

Think About It

- Why do you think Jesus taught so much about hell?

Day 67

JESUS SPEAKS ON ETERNITY

2 Corinthians 5:20–21; 1 Peter 2:21–25

In Matthew 25:46, Jesus discusses the two futures of everlasting life and eternal punishment. He uses the same adjective, *eternal*, for each one. Both heaven and hell are eternal—forever. Elsewhere, Jesus states clearly that hell is a place where "the fire is not quenched" (Mark 9:48). And Revelation says the wicked are punished "for ever and ever" (Revelation 14:11; 20:10). Every sin is an offense against the infinite God, and the penalty for that sin is also infinite. That is why the only one who can pay for our infinite debt is God's Son, Jesus (2 Corinthians 5:21; 1 Peter 2:24).

As the Son of God who knows all things, Jesus clearly warns us that hell is a horrible reality (Matthew 8:10–12; 25:31–46; Luke 13:24–28). Hell was one reason why Jesus was willing to humble himself and suffer for us on the cross. Jesus wants to save us from ourselves—from our own rebellion against God and its tragic consequences.

Need to Know

- The Greek word *aionos* is the word used for "everlasting" and "eternal" in Matthew 25:46, denoting a duration of undefined time, but refers to persons or things which are endless in their nature.

- The significance of Jesus' sacrifice turns on his sinlessness. He was the pure Lamb of God, the one who lived according to the true law of God. The sinless one paid the price for our sins.

Think About It

- How do you feel about Jesus' teachings about hell?
- Why is sin so abhorrent to God?

—— Day 68 ——

STANDING BEFORE GOD

Matthew 7:16–20; Matthew 12:35–37; John 5:24–29

Everyone—the living and the dead, people as well as angels—will stand before Christ (Hebrews 12:23; 1 Peter 4:5; Jude 6) to be judged according to the things they have done (Matthew 16:27; Romans 2:6; Revelation 22:12). Nothing can be hidden from God, not even our "secret thoughts" (Romans 2:16 CEV). Every deed will be examined, from idle words to not helping the hungry (Matthew 12:36; 25:31–46).

Because everyone has sinned (Romans 3:23), God's judgment will fall on all people—from murderers (Revelation 21:8) to pious hypocrites (Matthew 23:29–33), to those who fail to help the poor (Matthew 25:31–46). Only those people who are saved by Jesus' redemptive work will escape God's punishment.

Christ, the Judge, has already suffered God's punishment for sin. Those who have faith in him are forgiven of their sins (John 3:18; 5:24; Romans 3:25; 2 Corinthians 5:21). And what God has already forgiven, he will not recall (Isaiah 43:25; Jeremiah 31:34). That's why believers in Christ may stand before the Lord without fear (Romans 8:33–34; Ephesians 5:27).

While our works cannot save us, they aren't unimportant to God (Philippians 3:9). Though no other foundation "can no man lay than that is laid, which is Jesus Christ" (1 Corinthians 3:11), our faith must be active in forgiveness, love, and good works (Matthew 7:17–19). These works are the basis for the believer's rewards (1 Corinthians 3:10–15).

Need to Know

- The word that Paul used in Romans 3:23 for *sin* means "to miss the mark, to fail in the duty."
- God has set a standard for us to live up to. Jesus came to give us an example. We may rightly concentrate on singular behaviors that we call sin, but our sin is the failure to live up to God's expectations of us. Jesus spanned the gap between our failures and those expectations.

Think About It

- When you think of standing before God, what comes first to mind?

Day 69

WILL SOME SUFFER MORE THAN OTHERS?

Ephesians 2:4–10; Revelation 20:11–15

Describing the Lord's final judgment on the lost, Revelation 20:12 says, "The dead were judged out of those things which were written in the books, according to their works." The suggestion here is that Christ will consider people's earthly works before he passes final judgment on them. We know that works can do nothing to save a person (Ephesians 2:8–9). We also know that only lost people will be gathered at the great white throne judgment in Revelation 20. Therefore, it seems reasonable to conclude that Christ will impose different degrees of punishment based on people's works. Christ is a completely righteous and just Judge; he will assign each person the exact punishment he or she deserves.

Need to Know

- Humanity is created in God's image, and therefore all are morally accountable to God in a way that no other part of creation is.
- It is not humanity's guilt that will be decided at the last judgment. We are all guilty. What will be decided is whether we have accepted the redemption in Christ which God offers.

Think About It

- What kind of behaviors do you think will receive the harshest punishment?
- Do you feel free from fear of judgment?

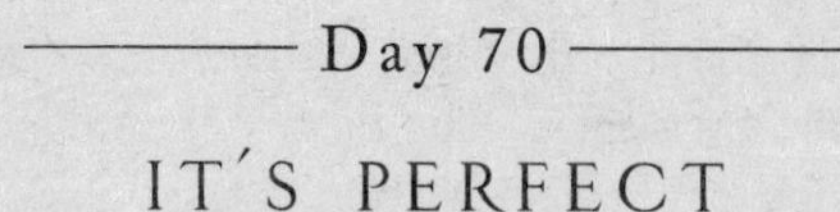

Day 70

IT'S PERFECT

Isaiah 65:17–19; John 14:1–4; Revelation 21:1–4

When scripture uses the word *heaven*, it may mean the whole cosmos, the sky (the realm of the planets and stars), or God's dwelling place. But when scripture describes the place where believers will live for eternity as *heaven*, it's referring to God's dwelling place. Jesus went to God's dwelling place, to stand in a position of authority beside God the Father (Acts 7:55–56). There, he is preparing a glorious place for all those who believe in him (John 14:2–3).

Following the final judgment and the defeat of all evil, God will create "a new heaven and a new earth" because the old earth and the old universe will have disappeared (Isaiah 65:17; 2 Peter 3:10; Revelation 21:1). Then, the place that Jesus has prepared for us—the New Jerusalem—will descend from the sky onto the new earth. In this sparkling, new city, God will finally live among his holy people. The New Jerusalem will be God's new dwelling place, and we will live with God in that city forever (Revelation 22:5).

Need to Know

- It was King David that made Jerusalem the spiritual center as well as the political capital city of Judah. The city had already existed as the city of Jebus.
- Some Christians see this New Jerusalem as a literal city. Others, just as convinced of God's judgment and restoration, see the New Jerusalem as the church of Christ, finally perfected when Christ returns.

Think About It

- In what way does the modern church feel weary and tired, ready for a spiritual overhaul into a new creation?
- What hope does it give you to think of a new world restored by God?

Fast Facts

The holy city is called the new Jerusalem
Its overall appearance is made of gray quartz (jasper) and pure gold
The city is shaped like a huge equilateral cube
The size of the structure is about 1,400 miles on each side
The foundation of the city is composed of twelve layers of stones inlaid with jewels
The names of each of the twelve apostles are engraved on the foundation layers
The walls around the city are built of gray quartz
The walls are over 200 feet high
There are twelve solid pearl gates (three on each wall)
Each gate is named for one the Israel's twelve tribes
The river of life flows in the city
The tree of life grows in the city
The throne room of God occupies the central palace
The city's main street is made of transparent gold
The dazzling light of the city comes from God's glory
God himself will live in the city among his people
God's people will live in the New Jerusalem in the presence of God's forever

Revelation 21:2
Revelation 21:11, 18
Revelation 21:16
Revelation 21:16
Revelation 21:14
Revelation 21:19–20
Revelation 21:18
Revelation 21:17
Revelation 21:12, 21
Revelation 21:12
Revelation 22:1
Revelation 2:7; 22:2
Revelation 4:2; 22:1
Revelation 21:21
Revelation 21:11, 23; 22:5
Revelation 21:3; 22:4
Revelation 22:5

Day 71

THE NEW JERUSALEM

Revelation 21:11–21

Do you ever yearn for true peace in your family, in your community, or in your nation? Do you dream of the day when you can finally put away your frantic work and truly rest? These hopes and longings will only be satisfied in heaven. Only in heaven will we be able to truly rest—to simply enjoy our Creator's presence. As John's images of golden streets, foundations of precious jewels and gates of pearl suggest, the New Jerusalem will be far beyond anything we have experienced or imagined. It will be a place of eternal joy and happiness—a place scripture calls the heavenly Jerusalem (Hebrews 12:22; 13:14).

In this heavenly Jerusalem, "there shall be no more curse" (Revelation 22:3). Just as God was present with Adam and Eve before the fall, so in the New Jerusalem God will dwell among his people (Revelation 21:3). All evil is eliminated in the New Jerusalem, and the possibility of sin is erased (Jude 24; Revelation 21:27). There is no "sorrow, nor crying" (Revelation 21:4). We will never be hungry or thirsty again (Revelation 7:16). Without the sinful hurdles of our present age, we will finally experience life as it's meant to be experienced, forever and ever (Revelation 22:1–2).

Need to Know

- The Old Testament prophet Isaiah gave a description similar to John's when he prophesied Jerusalem's restoration. He spoke of an eventual city made of precious jewels and filled with peace (Isaiah 54:11–14).
- In this New Jerusalem God will be the source of light, and Jesus, the Lamb, will be the lamp that sheds that light (Revelation 21:23).

Think About It

- How do you think your relationship and interactions with God will be different in the New Jerusalem?
- What experiences of your life have given you a little glimpse of what heaven will be?

Day 72

WHAT WILL HEAVEN BE LIKE?

Revelation 4:1–8

John provides a fantastic and rather baffling description of heaven and the throne of God in Revelation 4. It's certainly possible that John's depiction can be taken literally. Heaven may very well be a place of emerald rainbows, gold crowns, and a crystal sea. After all, God is capable of creating anything he desires. More likely, though, John was simply using the limited descriptive words and images available to him to communicate heaven's indescribable appearance.

All beauty comes from God. Anything that corrupts or taints beauty is the result of sin. So absolute beauty—breathtaking spectacle beyond our wildest imagination—will abound throughout heaven. "But as it is written, Eye hath not seen, nor ear heard, neither have entered into the heart of man, the things which God hath prepared for them that love him" (1 Corinthians 2:9).

Need to Know

- John was a Jewish man. His visions were certainly influenced by the visions of the Old Testament prophets Isaiah and Ezekiel. The writings of these men also contain otherworldly visions of God with his angels (Isaiah 6:1–4; Ezekiel 1:4–21).
- Some see the creatures surrounding God as angelic beings of a sort. Others see them as symbolic personifications of God's attributes: his all-knowing nature and his holiness.

Think About It

- Think about John's scenario of heavenly worship. Where do you see yourself in that scenario?
- How can we, through faith, accept the reality of a place and time that scripture itself says we can't imagine?

Day 73

IN HIS PRESENCE

1 Corinthians 13:11–12; Revelation 7:9–12

The Bible provides few glimpses of the believer's life in heaven. However, three themes dominate what we do know—worship, community, and service. They reflect God's original goal for humans before Adam and Eve's sin.

God created us to have a relationship with him (Genesis 1:26–27; 3:8). Throughout Revelation, heaven is portrayed as a place of unending praise for Jesus (Revelation 5:8–14; 7:9–12). We will no longer worship Jesus through the eyes of faith. Instead, we will see God's glory and will be filled with unspeakable joy (1 Corinthians 13:12; 2 Corinthians 5:7; 1 Peter 1:8; Revelation 22:3–4). God himself will illuminate the New Jerusalem, our eternal home, so that everyone will reflect the Lord's glory and be changed into his image (2 Corinthians 3:18; Revelation 21:23; 22:5).

Need to Know

- Throughout the scriptures, "seeing God" is represented as a potentially fatal endeavor. God hid Moses in the cleft of a mountain so that Moses wouldn't be completely exposed to God's face (Exodus 33:18–23). This gives some insight into the changes that will have taken place in heaven, where we will be in God's presence with no separation between us.

- Part of being in a relationship with God means being changed. The New Testament writers spoke often of our sanctification, the gradual molding to God's character revealed through Jesus (Romans 8:29). The reality of heaven will be that God will have completed that work in us.

Think About It

- How do you imagine your life in eternity?
- From what in this life do you most look forward to being redeemed?

Day 74

WILL HEAVEN BE ALL IT'S CRACKED UP TO BE?

John 14:1–7

Most people have probably entertained, at least briefly, the possibility that heaven may not be the place of eternal happiness we're led to believe it is. Biblical depictions of worshiping and praising God for eternity do not necessarily coincide with our notions of enjoyable activities. Perhaps this is due to the fact that our attitudes concerning enjoyment and boredom are tainted by our limited earthly experiences. The truth is, we have absolutely no concept, no way of imagining, the pleasure and fulfillment that awaits us in heaven. Think of it this way: Not only is heaven a place prepared especially for us (John 14:2–4), it is also the place where God himself has chosen to dwell forever!

Need to Know

- It is difficult for us, bound in time that passes moment by moment, to imagine being in a realm in which time does not exist. We measure life's passing by the setting of the sun and the aging of our bodies. In the afterlife, those two things will not exist. We will be in a state of being with God, rather than a state of trying to get somewhere else.
- We think of heaven as the place where God dwells, but we must not forget that the work of Jesus paved the way for God's dwelling place to be within us. Heaven will be wonderful, but we don't have to wait for it to live in the presence of God now.

Think About It

- What kind of fulfillment do you expect in heaven that you haven't found in this life?
- How do your views of heaven differ today from your views as a child?

Day 75

LET'S CELEBRATE!

1 Corinthians 15:35–44; Revelation 19:7–9

God's plan for people to exist in community (Genesis 1:27; 2:18) is fulfilled in heaven. One of Jesus' favorite metaphors to describe heaven is that of a wedding banquet, where everyone is eagerly welcomed and befriended (Matthew 22:2–14). Heaven will be a party that no one will want to leave. Revelation eagerly looks forward to this great wedding feast, which will celebrate the perfect union of Jesus and his church (Revelation 19:7–9). Believers are bound by such fellowship and love that together we are portrayed as Christ's bride. What an image of community!

In heaven, we will have glorified bodies (1 Corinthians 15:35–50). We will use these new bodies to serve God's kingdom. In a sense, God will be restoring us to our intended purpose, for he created Adam and Eve to serve him by cultivating the earth (Genesis 1:26, 28; Psalm 8:1–9). Jesus promises that we will be given authority to serve the kingdom in the future, even to reign as kings (Matthew 19:28–30; Revelation 2:26–27; 22:5). In the New Jerusalem, there will be new, exciting opportunities for learning, developing, and unfolding God's creation for his glory.

Need to Know

- The New Testament writers had just witnessed a change from an earthly body to a heavenly body—Jesus Christ. His body had changed enough that not everyone recognized him immediately, and he admonished Mary not to touch him (John 20:15–17). Yet he looked the same enough for them to eventually recognize who he was and relate to him as the Jesus they had known.
- When Jesus told the disciples that they would eventually rule with him, he made another wonderful promise as well. He promised that anyone who had given up anything because of their faith, would be paid back one hundred times the value of what they had lost (Matthew 19:29).

Think About It

- What do you see as your God-given responsibilities in this world to prepare for the next?

Day 76

WILL I LOOK DIFFERENT IN HEAVEN?

John 20:13–21

First, let's dispel some popular notions about our heavenly appearance and activity. Nowhere does scripture describe citizens of heaven as sporting wings and halos, floating around on fluffy white clouds, or playing harps.

Contrary to another popular notion, we won't be mere spirits or ghosts in heaven. Jesus will raise our bodies from the dead and, after that, will determine our eternal destinies. At that time, we will have real, physical bodies, like that of the risen Christ. When Christ rose from the dead, he could eat. People even touched him (John 20–21). Yet his body was different somehow; it was transformed. This renewed, transformed body is what believers have to look forward to in heaven.

Need to Know

- Until he spoke her name, Mary Magdalene didn't recognize Jesus' transformed body after his resurrection. The two disciples on the road to Emmaus (Luke 24:15–16) also failed to recognize Jesus while they were with him, though they visited with him for quite some time.
- When Jesus appeared to the disciples, they thought him to be a spirit. He convinced them he was real by eating fish and honeycomb (Luke 24:33–41).

Think About It

- What are the popular notions you hear about heaven?
- One day God will transform your body. In what way, today, is he transforming your soul?

Day 77

USE WISDOM

Revelation 20:4–6, 12–13

Some people are hard to read. You can't tell when they're joking and when they're being serious. As a result, it's difficult to know when to accept their words at face value and when to take them with a grain of salt. The book of Revelation presents a similar problem. Bible scholars disagree as to how much of the book should be interpreted literally and how much should be viewed as symbolism. No passages in Revelation have inspired more controversy than those dealing with bodily resurrection (Revelation 20:4–6, 12–13).

We need to approach difficult texts like Revelation 20:4–6 with humility and caution. God's ways are above our own. But despite all the different interpretations of this passage, each end-times view confesses the return of Christ, a future bodily resurrection, a final judgment, and a new heaven and new earth. We know Jesus will one day return in glory to establish a better and perfect place.

Need to Know

- There are differing opinions of who is sitting on the thrones assisting in God's judgment. Some think they are the martyrs for the faith. Others think they are the twenty-four elders or even the twelve disciples. No one knows for sure.

- People who do not believe in a literal thousand-year reign interpret the first resurrection to be the spiritual resurrection we experience at the time of our salvation.

Think About It

- What is most important to you about Christ's return?
- What principles do you use to understand passages that people interpret many different ways?

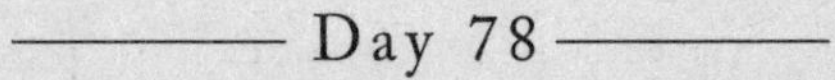

Day 78

AMILLENNIALISM: ONE RESURRECTION

John 12:31; Romans 6:6–11; Revelation 20:1–3

Amillennialists believe in only one general resurrection at the end of this age. The book of Revelation, they observe, consists of visions that portray God's work throughout the entire church age. So Revelation 20:1–3 symbolically describes Jesus' binding of Satan during his earthly ministry (Matthew 12:29; John 12:31; Colossians 2:15). The Millennium, then, symbolizes the church age.

According to this view, the first resurrection, described in Revelation 20:6, refers to a person's salvation (Ezekiel 37:1–14; Romans 6:6–11; Ephesians 2:1, 5). Note that John refers to the "souls" of the martyrs, not their bodies (Revelation 20:4), suggesting a new spiritual existence. Revelation concludes that "the second death," or hell, "has no power over" those experiencing this first resurrection (Revelation 20:6 CEV; 21:8). The vision of the church age ends with a physical resurrection of all the dead for final judgment (Revelation 20:12–13).

Need to Know

- Resurrection has been a hot topic since the time of Christ, even before his resurrection. What set the Sadducees apart as religious leaders in Jesus' day was their doctrine that beyond death there is no resurrection.
- The church age refers to age in which we are living right now, as the church and body of Christ.

Think About It

- What seems most important to you about the final reign of Christ, even in the midst of so many differing opinions about the logistics of it?
- You are living in the church age. What do you think are the most significant contributions of the church in the present age?

Day 79

POSTMILLENNIALISM: ONE RESURRECTION

Revelation 20:4–10

Postmillennialists believe in a future age of spiritual prosperity for the church. They contend that the bodily resurrection for the righteous and the wicked occurs at Jesus' second coming.

Postmillennialists interpret the book of Revelation as a set of visions that reiterate God's work. They believe the final set of visions begins in Revelation 19:11 with the conquering Lamb slaying his enemies through the sword of his mouth. This supports their view that the Word of God will triumph over all opposition and establish a period of spiritual prosperity.

While the vision shifts in Revelation 20:4–6, the opening battle between God and Satan determines its context. John sees the raised souls of those who are martyred "for the witness of Jesus." Postmillennialists point out that while these souls reign with Christ, the text never states that Christ is present on earth. Postmillennialists interpret Revelation 20:4–6 as a vision of the Christian martyrs who are present with Christ in the "intermediate state." They are with Christ. They're rejoicing that Christ's cause has triumphed and that they won't go to hell (Philippians 1:23; Revelation 20:6; 21:8). So postmillennialists believe the second resurrection at the end of the Millennium is a physical resurrection of everyone to face God's final judgment.

Need to Know

- The "intermediate state" is the period of waiting for those who have died before the second coming and are yet to be resurrected with Christ. The parable of the rich man and Lazarus offers some foundation when interpreted literally (Luke 16:19–31).

Think About It

- Do you agree or disagree with the postmillennialist view?
- As you observe the points of your own faith, for what would you be willing to be martyred?

Day 80

PREMILLENNIALISM: TWO RESURRECTIONS

Daniel 12:2–4; Luke 20:34–38; 1 Thessalonians 4:14–18

Premillennialists believe that Christ, at the Second Coming, resurrects dead believers to reign with him through the Millennium. After that, the rest of the dead are raised for the final judgment.

Premillennialists interpret Revelation 19:11–20:15 literally. In this vision of Armageddon, the conquering Lamb descends to earth and triumphs over his enemies (Revelation 19:13). Believers are raised to participate in Christ's reign on earth for one thousand years, after which the rest of the dead are raised.

Premillennialists point to Revelation 20:4–5 to support their belief in two bodily resurrections. The same Greek word *ezesan* ("lived" or "came back to life") is used to refer to the believers who come back to life before the Millennium and the remaining dead who return to life after the Millennium. Premillennialists point out that other scripture passages suggest a two-stage bodily resurrection: first the righteous and then the wicked (Daniel 12:2; Luke 14:14; 20:35; 1 Thessalonians 4:16).

Need to Know

- In the premillennialist's view, there is a second and a third coming of Christ. In the second coming, Jesus secretly steals aways believers. Then, in the third, he returns in the sight of all to judge mankind.
- Jesus was resurrected to an eternal state. There were other resurrections in the Bible though—Lazarus (John 11), the daughter of Jairus (Luke 8) for instance—that were merely resurrections back to temporary life. There were also resurrections at the time of Jesus' resurrection. Matthew 27:50–53 tells us that many of the dead rose and appeared in the surrounding cities. All these people still faced eventual death.

Think About It

- How would you live your life differently were there no resurrection?
- How would you define the hope of the resurrection?

Day 81

WHAT WILL BEING RAISED FROM THE DEAD BE LIKE?

John 11:32–44

The resurrection of believers is a physical, rather than merely a spiritual, event. The raising of Lazarus (John 11:38–44) and the Lord himself (Luke 24:36–39)—both of whom returned from the dead physically—serve as "previews" of the resurrection of believers.

The apostle Paul tells us that when Jesus returns, "the dead in Christ shall rise first" (1 Thessalonians 4:16). The event will be announced by the voice of the archangel and the blast of a trumpet. Immediately after the dead are raised, those believers who are still living will ascend to meet Jesus in the air (1 Thessalonians 4:17). What an exciting day that will be!

Need to Know

- Paul marks Christ's second coming with three signs: a shout, the call of the archangel, and the trumpet of God. These could be three distinct sounds or descriptions of the same sound.
- An archangel is an angel appointed to a certain task. If there is a developed hierarchy of angels, this would be an angel high in rank. Michael was called an archangel (Jude 9).

Think About It

- What do you believe about angels interacting with your everyday life?

- When you imagine suddenly hearing a sound that means the end has come, what do you think and feel?

Day 82

ANGELS

Luke 2:8–14; Revelation 5:11–12

From television shows to greeting cards, angels have flown into our collective cultural heart. The yearning to be "touched by an angel" often reflects a desire to connect to some higher power or to "find one's self." But is that the purpose of angels? Do they exist simply to enhance our well-being?

Scripture tells us that angels are spiritual beings created by God to serve him in various capacities. As members of God's heavenly courts, angels number in the "thousands of thousands" (Revelation 5:11). When angels appear on earth, they often reflect their heavenly status through their dazzling radiance. Their appearance can terrify people (Luke 2:9; Revelation 4:5; 10:1).

Need to Know

- There are only two angels actually named in the Bible—Gabriel and Michael (and perhaps Satan, depending on how you view his origination).
- In the Old Testament, it is sometimes hard to tell

whether an angel has appeared or a form of God himself, referred to as an "angel of the Lord."

Think About It

- Have you ever had an experience or heard of an experience that seemed to be somehow related to a modern-day interaction with an angel?
- Would you be terrified if an angel appeared to you with a message from God? What would it take to convince you it was really an angel from God?

Day 83

WHAT ANGELS DO

Psalm 103:19–22; Psalm 148:1–5

The primary task of angels is to praise God (Psalm 103:20; 148:1–2; Daniel 7:10). The sheer number and awesome worship of the angelic host affirm God's infinite glory (Isaiah 6:3; Revelation 5:11–13). In heaven Satan coveted this type of worship for himself, and his rebellion led other angels to fall as well. So now angels are divided into two groups: the righteous and the wicked. The wicked angels, demons, were defeated when Jesus died on the cross. God will eventually condemn them to the lake of fire (Matthew 25:41; Colossians 2:15). The righteous angels, on the other hand, are instrumental in God's battle against evil.

Need to Know

- Angels—righteous and wicked—are created beings with limitations. They are neither omniscient nor omnipresent.
- Each of the seven churches addressed in the first three chapters of Revelation was addressed through an angel. There are a variety of interpretations of the identity of these angels.

Think About It

- Given the choice of whether to be an angel of God or a redeemed child of God, which would you choose?
- The primary task of angels is to praise God. How would you define your primary task before God?

——— Day 84 ———

ANGELS DO GOD'S WORK

Matthew 4:10–11; Matthew 28:2–7; Acts 5:19–20

Angels not only announced the birth of the Messiah (Luke 1:5–38; 2:8–20), they were also the first to proclaim Jesus' victory over death (Matthew 28:2–7). They prodded the church to spread the Good News of Christ to non-Jews and the leaders of the world (Acts 5:19; 8:26; 10:3–8, 22; 27:23–24). Revelation suggests this same role for angels in the end times.

Angels are responsible for leading the church to proclaim the Good News "to every nation, and kindred, and tongue, and people" (Revelation 10:7; 14:6–7, 9–11).

Angels ministered to Jesus throughout his time on earth, particularly during such difficult circumstances as his temptation and his moment of decision in Gethsemane (Matthew 4:11; Mark 1:13; Luke 22:43). The angels provided strength for Jesus, bringing him food during the forty days of his temptation and spiritually comforting him. Scripture promises that angels will help believers as well (Hebrews 1:14). In Revelation, the angels of the seven churches fulfill this role by communicating God's praise as well as God's rebuke to believers (Revelation 2:1–3:22).

Need to Know

- In the Bible, angels typically appeared familiar enough to be accepted by people, but different enough—extremely white or light—to give them credence as creatures outside of this world (Matthew 28:3).
- Angelology is the doctrine of angels. Angels are not of major study in Christian theology, but recognized as playing a role in much of God's work throughout human history. Paul warned the Colossian Christians to refrain from worshiping angels (Colossians 2:18–19).

Think About It

- If you could ask an angel any question, what would it be?

- What message do you need to receive from God in this season of your life?

——— Day 85 ———

ANGELS OF WRATH

Matthew 13:37–43, 47–51

Jesus promised that angels would accompany him at the Second Coming and help separate the wicked from the righteous at the final judgment (Matthew 13:41, 49; 25:31; Mark 8:38). Revelation details this role of angels as the emissaries of the conquering Lamb's judgment. When the Lamb opens the seals to unleash God's wrath on the wicked (Revelation 5–6), the angels typically summon these judgments and often personally carry them out (Revelation 6:1–7; 7:2–3; 14:14–20; 16:1–21; 20:1–3). For instance, the seventh angel pours out the vial of God's fierce anger on Babylon, producing an earthquake that causes mountains to dissolve and the city to be "divided into three parts" (Revelation 16:17–20).

Need to Know

- The seals were attached to scrolls. An angel asked, Who could open the scrolls by breaking the seals? Jesus, the Lamb, was the only one worthy.
- The vials, or bowls, of judgment and their resulting plagues came on the heels of other judgments. First,

the plagues from the seals destroyed a fourth of the earth. Then the trumpets brought judgments that destroyed another third of the earth. The seven bowls (vials), poured by seven angels, were directed toward the antichrist's followers but also affected what remained of the earth.

Think About It

- The seals, the trumpets, and the bowls—all symbols of judgment. What best symbolizes God's judgment in your life?
- How much of your initiative in obeying God is prompted by judgment?

Day 86

UNDER JESUS' COMMAND

Ephesians 1:17–23; Colossians 2:16–19; 1 Peter 3:18–22

While angels are an integral part of scripture's vision of the end times, they always serve Jesus. Angels had absolutely no part in saving us. Revelation's account of the warfare between God's angels and Satan does not suggest that the angels achieve victory on their own. Rather, Satan isn't strong enough to defeat the angels because of the "blood of the lamb" (Revelation 12:11). The angels do fight Satan and his demons (Daniel 10:10–13; Revelation 12:7–12), but Christ directs the battle and delivered that final, defeating blow to Satan when he died on the cross. So the angels are more like privates in Jesus' heavenly army. They're more like ring-side attendants at a boxing match. They remove the defeated from the ring. Jesus alone is the conquering Lamb. Jesus alone defeats Satan once and for all!

Jesus is supreme over all angelic beings. The angels were created to serve him (Ephesians 1:20–22; 1 Peter 3:22). Any angel who diverts attention from Jesus belongs to Satan's camp, for Jesus alone should receive our worship (Colossians 2:18; Revelation 22:8–9). We must not let our culture's fascination with angels divert our attention from the only one who can save: Jesus Christ!

Need to Know

- Angels do not marry and do not die (Luke 20:34–36). They are not a race descended from others, but rather a group created by God, probably genderless.
- At Jesus' ascension it was two angels who announced to the crowd that Jesus would return the same way (Acts 1:10–11).

Think About It

- Besides angels, what else does our culture focus on rather than Jesus for the source of spirituality?
- What things in your life function as rivals for Christ's supremacy?

Day 87

REWARDS

Matthew 7:15–20; Galatians 6:7–10

Scripture promises that Christ will judge all people on the basis of their works at the final judgment. Even the judgment of believers will focus on works because our faith must be active in forgiveness, in love, and in good works. After all, a good tree bears good fruit (Matthew 7:17–19; Galatians 5:6; James 2:26). Scripture promises not only that God has saved us for good works, but also that he will reward whatever good we do (see Ephesians 6:8; 1 Corinthians 3:11–15; 9:16–27; 2 Corinthians 5:10; Galatians 6:7–10; Ephesians 2:10; 1 Peter 5:1–4).

Need to Know

- We think of being rewarded for something good and punished for something bad. The word *reward* actually applies to both. You will receive the appropriate reward for your actions, whether it is positive or negative.
- The writer of Ecclesiastes noted that we can't expect rewards in this life. Sometimes in this life the righteous suffer and the wicked prosper. We must trust God to reward our faith in his time (Ecclesiastes 7:14–17).

Think About It

- What kind of spiritual fruit does your life bear?

• As you evaluate your own life, do good works pour out of your sincere faith?

Day 88

PAUL'S TEACHING ON REWARDS

Matthew 6:1–4; 1 Corinthians 3:11–17

The apostle Paul explained the concept of rewards in more detail. While he emphatically affirms that Christ is the only foundation for our salvation, various structures can be erected on that foundation. Some structures are made of gold and precious stones; others are made of hay and straw. On the day of judgment, these structures will be tested by fire. "If any man's work abide which he hath built thereupon, he shall receive a reward. If any man's work shall be burned, he shall suffer loss" (1 Corinthians 3:14–15). This does not imply damnation, because the person "shall be saved; yet so as by fire" (1 Corinthians 3:15). Both builders are saved, but only the one whose building survives receives a reward. If the motive for one's works is self-glory and not the glory of God, the result is loss. Likewise, if one's motive is seeking the praise of people, there will be no reward from God (Matthew 6:1).

Need to Know

• Jesus told the story of a man who built his house on

rock and one who built his house on sand. When the storms came, the house built on rock was the only one that withstood (Matthew 7:24–27). Often our rewards are the consequences of our actions.

- Another way to look at rewards is sowing and reaping. This concept is woven throughout scripture, from Job's friend Eliphaz (Job 4:8), to the writer of the Proverbs (Proverbs 22:8), to Paul the apostle (2 Corinthians 9:6).

Think About It

- What are you sowing spiritually, and what will you reap from it?
- What reward do you think you'll receive from God?

Day 89

WHY ARE CROWNS IMPORTANT?

2 Corinthians 3:18; Ephesians 2:10; 2 Timothy 4:7–8; Revelation 3:11

What are these rewards that the Bible depicts as crowns (1 Corinthians 9:25; Revelation 2:10; 3:11)? Scripture describes them simply as the virtues of being like Christ. The "crown of glory that fadeth not away" (1 Peter 5:4) refers to the fact that we will reflect Christ's own image of God's glory (2 Corinthians 3:18). The crown of righteousness (2 Timothy 4:8) refers to Christ's righteousness, which we will embody in the future (Romans 8:3–4; Ephesians 2:10). The prize of rejoicing in other believers (Philippians 4:1; 1 Thessalonians 2:19) reflects Christ's kingdom of reconciling love. The eternal "crown of life" (James 1:12; Revelation 2:10) refers to communion with Christ forever. In other words, these prizes are the characteristics of the Christian life.

Need to Know

- In the Old Testament crowns symbolized a specialty or specialized task. Priests wore crowns marked, "holy to the Lord." Hebrew kings wore simple crowns that could be worn into battle. Wreaths of flowers were also worn as crowns in celebrations.
- Jesus' crown of thorns was a parody of a victor's wreath—a laurel wreath worn as an honor—used to shame and disdain him.

Think About It

- How do you respond to the idea that our crowns will be our Christlikeness?
- In what ways can you see that God is making you like Christ?

Day 90

REWARDED ACCORDING TO OUR WORKS

Luke 19:12–27; Revelation 4:4, 10–11

Many premillennialists also connect these rewards with reigning in Christ's millennial kingdom (Luke 22:30; 1 Corinthians 6:2–3; 2 Timothy 2:12; Revelation 20:4). Several of Jesus' parables suggest that he will offer the reward of ruling to the faithful when he returns (Matthew 25:14–30; Luke 19:12–27). Amillennialists interpret this reward as increased responsibility in the new earth (Revelation 5:9–10), new opportunities for learning and cultivating God's creation for his glory.

Believers will be rewarded for their good works at the day of judgment. But by their very nature, these crowns nurture and intensify our attempts to be like Christ. These rewards won't bring attention to the person who receives it, but will ultimately bring glory to God. Like the white-robed leaders described in Revelation 4:4, believers will cast their crowns before Christ, praising God, "Thou art worthy, O Lord, to receive glory and honour and power" (Revelation 4:11).

Need to Know

- In the parable of Luke 19, the nobleman left for a time. If Jesus represents the nobleman in the parable, which most agree he does, then the story makes the point that Jesus will be gone for a time, leaving the world in our hands to run it well.

- The Greek word used here for *crowns* denotes a victor's crown or honor for distinguished service. Any and all honor we receive from God will be offered back to him who is worthy of all praise.

Think About It

- How do you use the resources God's given you by investing them wisely?
- How would you like to be living differently in light of the reality that you will stand before God one day?